PRAISE FOR *UNPOLISHED GEM*

'Delightful – a funny, touching debut.' *Courier Mail*

'There's something striking on every page.'
Helen Garner

'Virtuoso storytelling' *The Australian*

—

PRAISE FOR *HER FATHER'S DAUGHTER*

'Pung has an extraordinary story to tell and the finesse to
bring it, most movingly, to the page.' *The Monthly*

'A beautiful exploration of father–daughter relationships.' *Vogue*

'Remarkably tender and thoughtful' *The Sunday Age*

—

PRAISE FOR *LAURINDA*

'Biting yet compassionate' *Australian Book Review*

'Funny, horrifying and sharp as a serpent's fangs.' John Marsden

'A candid and powerful exploration of family, culture and class.'
Readings Monthly

'Exquisitely sharp' *The Age*

—

PRAISE FOR *ON JOHN MARSDEN*

'A timely reminder of the value of authentic representation
in literature and the power of being seen.' *ArtsHub*

'There is deep love and respect in her words.' *AU Review*

CLOSE TO HOME

CLOSE TO HOME

SELECTED WRITINGS

ALICE PUNG

Published by Black Inc.,
an imprint of Schwartz Publishing Pty Ltd
Level 1, 221 Drummond Street
Carlton VIC 3053, Australia
enquiries@blackincbooks.com
www.blackincbooks.com

9781760640910 (paperback)
9781743820582 (ebook)

A catalogue record for this
book is available from the
National Library of Australia

Cover design by Jen Clark
Text design and typesetting by Marilyn de Castro
Cover photograph of author at the Little Saigon Market in 2008
by Simon Schluter / Fairfax Syndication
Back cover photograph of author © Courtney Brown 2018

For Nick

CONTENTS

STEALING FROM LITTLE SAIGON

STEALING FROM LITTLE SAIGON

My mother knows a certain marketplace in Melbourne the same way some people know their spouses. She comes from two generations of traders. She knows all the different ways to get around any market, how to coax, control, cajole and conquer: all the tricks of the trade. My great-grandmother hawked boiled eggs on the streets of Phnom Penh, her own mother sold fried rice-and-chive cakes before Pol Pot came, and when they were exiled in Vietnam, my mother sold fabric in a Saigon stall.

This market is called Little Saigon, and my mother shops here twice a week. If you walked inside and paid no heed to the outside world, you could very well be in Vietnam. It has white tiles on the floor, and a number of different stalls selling everything from durian cakes and roast ducks to jewellery and rice-bowl-shaped bras. There are also two large supermarkets of the non-chain variety selling fresh produce, including over five different types of mushroom — enoki, shiitake, oyster, Korean and standard brown. One of the supermarkets carries swimming, crawling seafood in tanks. In any other suburb, a market with this sort of fare would be considered an exotic place for gourmands, with the prices handwritten on squares of cardboard with neat black frames, beneath the one-sentence description of the obscure comestible. But not here. Here, you can get mangoes for three dollars a kilo.

The name says everything you need to know about the migrants who run the place – what era they come from, what government they were living under before they left, and their nostalgic yearnings towards some point in the past. In many ways, our lives revolve around the marketplace, and from an outsider's view, our parents seem to be trying to replicate the patterns of their youth in Phnom Penh. These are people who bury gold in their backyards and buy three-day-old buns from the bakery. All their lives have been about sequestering things away so that no one can see how much they have, in case forces more powerful – governments, soldiers, the snaking coils of family nepotism gone poisonous – take what they have. Humility, hard work and an overvigilant sense of privacy: that's what they now believe in.

However, the same values seem not to apply when it comes to scrutinising other people. One evening, my mother came home and told us about a woman in town whose husband was much older than her. My mother said she tried to keep out of things, but she couldn't help having ears. 'She's so young and she is looking after a decrepit old man,' the gossipmongers whispered to one another in the vegetable stall when they saw the wife leading her husband by the elbow and choosing tomatoes. In the jewellery stores, when the wife came to sell off some gold to pay for her husband's most recent hospital bill, they talked. In the bank, when she was lining up with him to collect his pension, they whispered.

One day, the odd couple came to the electrical appliance store where my mother worked, to buy an iron. 'My son is moving to work in Bendigo this year,' the wife told my mother, and all who were within earshot. 'He's become a doctor.'

'What a smart son you have!' my mother exclaimed. All the while wondering, as they all did, *exactly how large a gap is there between you and your husband?*

'He's smart, like his mother!' the old man chuckled. 'She was such a smart little girl. Did you know that when we were in the camp, she used to collect cola cans, and somehow she ended up making little chairs and tables from them.'

'We stayed for twelve years at the Thai refugee camp,' added his wife.

'Yes, and when the Red Cross white people and the Jesus white people came to set up their tents, they would be so charmed by her little tin furniture that they actually gave her some money for them! Hehehe.'

'Shut up, you.' She gave him a little push to his shoulder.

'Oi! Be careful you don't topple your old man over!'

'So, did you know each other at the camp?' my mother asked.

'We met at the camp,' the wife said.

'She was wandering around, like a little lost creature.'

'I was only twelve.'

'But as smart as a fox.'

'The Black Thieves smashed my parents,' said the wife – and of course my mother knew who the Black Thieves were; it was what they all called the Khmer Rouge in Cambodia – 'and then a cousin took me to the camp. He –' she pointed to her husband '– he was thirty years old. He had once worked for my parents back in Phnom Penh. He became my older brother. He looked after me when I was a small child in the camp for all those years, and so now it's my turn to look after him.'

It was then that my mother realised the woman wasn't so young, and her husband wasn't so old. Suffering had etched calligraphy lines of experience on his face, and he had alleviated as many of his wife's hardships as he could, which is probably why she looked the way she did.

*

Recently, my mother told us that she had seen a small bout of shoplifting at one of the two supermarkets in Little Saigon. While my mother was trying to buy some spinach, there was a loud yell. My mother looked towards the nectarine trestle table and saw that a cleaver-wielding man, eyes popping like a *dybbuk*, had grabbed hold of the wrist of a petrified young Indian woman with a long braid down her back. 'Thief! Thief!' he hollered. He held up a clear plastic bag containing a single mango. 'You haven't paid for this.'

'Yes, I have.'

'*Where* did you pay for this?'

'Over there.' She pointed to the furthermost counter.

'That's not our counter!'

The stalls were set up in such haphazard fashion that you could not tell where one market began and the other ended. If this was your first time, you would think that it was one enormous market, until you started to notice the counters.

Yet my mother had seen the young woman walking around the market with the mango in her bag for a while. The man led her to the correct counter, still clinging to the cleaver, which he used to cut open nectarines for customers to taste. 'Did she pay for this?'

'No,' yelled the cashier woman, 'she did not come here to pay.'

'We call the police!' declared the cleaver-wielding man.

The young Indian woman's eyebrows knotted and she looked like she was about to cry.

'Please don't call the police,' she begged, opening up her purse. 'I pay for it.'

'We call the police. You pay for it now.'

She took out some coins and handed them to the cashier.

'Twenty dollars, or we call police.'

'Twenty dollars?'

'Twenty dollars.'

'For one mango?'

'For you steal.'

'But I don't have twenty dollars.'

'Then wait here, we call police.' Grabbing her wrist, he took out his mobile phone with one hand.

'Okay, okay, I pay.'

*

The marketplace is a law unto itself, where moral cause-and-effect accumulates interest. The mores are simple, the sort of universal laws that one would find within the first ten or so precepts of every major faith and culture: don't steal, don't lie, don't cheat. A rigid and unassailable sense of morality comes with a certain level of comfort, perhaps: a conviction that life will not change, or that God will not blink or turn his face away. But these were not my mother's convictions. She had never believed in a compassionate God. She came from a country where women's throats were cut with palm leaves, and coconut juice had been used in intravenous drips as a blood substitute. Where people were still scrambling for food scraps on the floor. The kind of stealing my mother witnessed was not the happy frisson of high-school hijinks.

She knew it for what it was – it was a secret, this shame. Even though the trestle tables were so laden with fruit that every evening at six o'clock the market workers would stuff plastic bags and sell them for two dollars each, the Indian girl wasn't supposed to be trying to smuggle out that lump of fruit without having paid for it, just as my mother knew she wasn't supposed to have lied at the refugee camp to smuggle a seed of a different sort out. She was eight months pregnant with me when she arrived in Australia, and the only way she could get on that plane was to lie and say that she was four months along.

Perhaps it was similar to the sort of shame that made my parents afraid to ask for things, even from fifteen-year-olds behind the counter at McDonald's; they always got us to ask for the sweet-and-sour sauce for our nuggets, always berated us for our sullen reluctance. It was the petty avarice of the poor, and punished even more harshly by the migrants who had been here longer and who had achieved the enviable 'permanent resident' status, because this thievery reminded them of who they used to be, how they used to think and, occasionally, what they used to do.

I had seen it once myself, when I was leading an interviewer and filmmaker through Footscray Market, two blocks away from Little Saigon. Filmmakers who feel like they need an authentic visa into Footscray and the world of these migrants and their markets sometimes ask me to be their passports. Their genuine sense of decency cringes at filming poverty, but when led through the streets by a loquacious local guide, this suddenly becomes an adventure akin to those they had when they backpacked through Vietnam or Laos. I am the link between what is foreign – the market – and what is familiar – my made-in-Australia roots and lack of an Oriental accent.

That day, there was yelling in the middle of the fruit section. 'She come-a do this every week!' hollered the Mediterranean fruit-stall owner, who had his hand firmly on the vinyl-covered trolley of an old, stooped-over Asian grandma. He flung open the flap of her trolley to reveal a bunch of bananas and some potatoes. 'Come see! Come see!' he beckoned to the film crew. He wanted to catch the culprit on film, even though the documentary was about something else.

'Have pity on me,' the old woman cried in Cantonese, lifting up her trouser leg, 'my leg hurts.' Sure enough, her leg was bandaged from the sockless foot to the mid-calf. By then, a small circle of onlookers had formed around the Greek fruitier, the old-lady pilferer and her trolley.

'Here, here,' said one woman, handing the stall owner five dollars, 'take this! Take this! I pay for her.'

'No want your money!' He pushed the note aside. 'You no understand, she come-a do this every week!' He beckoned to the cameraman. 'Quick, put camera here!' he directed, as if he were running the show.

We quietly made our exit, leaving the little circle to disperse. As we walked away, I realised this: there I was, with a camera crew and books and words, and I knew that the people whose worlds I wrote about would never read my books, and the people who read my books would never fully inhabit these worlds, even though they have already begun to populate them. And when they do, increasing the property prices for those already living in Footscray, they will make the existing residents very happy because now they will be able to purchase a house-and-land package in the newly opened manicured feats of urban planning that lie just a Toyota Camry drive away from the countryside. And Mr and Ms Stall Owner will at last be able to move away from the hollering hot masses of fruit-pilfering new arrivals.

So I show my film crew strange fruit, and hope they quickly forget about the incident with the old lady. I show them how to dip slices of sour mango in dishes of salt and chilli. They look in astonishment at the cleaver-wielding hecklers. And then I take them to a pho restaurant for lunch. I don't mention how housewives will heave and clutch their hearts over being short-changed ten cents. I never mention the young Indian woman who once put a single mango in a plastic bag without paying for it. At the end of the day, they can leave and marvel over the interesting cultural tour. They do not see the missing fingers from meat slicers, the feet ruined by vats of hot oil accidentally spilled, the hacking coughs from inhaling the floating mites of polyester fibres.

The marketplace is a front, the final face of our lives – the most charismatic, enterprising and proud. And the most extraordinary thing the filmmakers will take away from the day, the only true thing I will disclose about my mother's market, and the one thing they will write about in the newspapers with wonder, is that it is possible to buy mangoes for three dollars a kilo.

STRAWBERRY FIELDS FOREVER

Every day is labour day for South-East Asian migrants, so the idea of Labour Day being a public holiday is ludicrous to my family. On holidays we generally clean the house, mop the floor, mow the lawn and do the myriad other things we don't get a chance to do during the normal working weekend. We make the most of our family time together: my siblings and I skate on the tiles with drying cloths tied to our feet and Mr Mop in our arms. My mother, hair tied back with a rubber band and her hands in a bucket of suds, hums old Chinese pop songs while my father, who can neither sing nor dance, lunges into the car with the Dustbuster.

But this particular Labour Day was different. 'Let's go pick stwawbellies,' my mother had suggested a few days earlier. 'The Teochew Chinese Friendship Association are organising a trip.'

'We've done that before,' protested my father.

'No, that was the chelly farm,' said my mother, rhyming cherries with jellies. 'These stwawbellies are meant to be big – bigger than supermarket ones.'

'Larger than the ones in the Little Saigon Market?'

'Old Mrs Teng said much bigger!'

We were already imagining fruit the size of small apples as we did a quick ring around of the extended family. My father appealed to their sense of parental self-sacrifice to convince them to take the day off work.

'A good trip for the kids,' he told his sister, 'and picking strawberries is safer than other fruit. They don't grow on trees that you can fall out of and die.'

On Labour Day morning my mother woke, as usual, at 6.30. By the time the rest of us rose, the picnic was packed: a loaf of Safeway bread, boxes of Barbecue Shapes (biscuits from the Arnott's factory where my uncle worked) and a purple 'picnic rug' (actually a plastic tablecloth my mother found on sale at Forges of Footscray). A Vietnamese pork loaf went into the icebox.

'Aww, not the icebox.'

We hated carrying the icebox and the two-litre bottle of Coke and the plastic cups. We also hated washing the ice so that it was no longer pork-flavoured. My parents packed their Lo Han Guo drink – half-tea, half-medicine, and commonly known as 'Chinese Coke' – in a stainless-steel Tiger flask.

My father also packed our Akubra hats. He had bought genuine Akubras for all of us, so we'd look like quality Australians and not stand out in a crowd. But my mother preferred her 'SONY – the One and Only' cap that came with our television, and my siblings preferred not to look like the Chinese *Crocodile Dundee* delegates. So my father was usually left holding all the hats; once he wore three, piled on top of one another, because he didn't want to carry them. He became a walking advertisement for Paul Ho Gan.

Piling into our Toyota LandCruiser that had never seen the bush, off we drove. Fifteen minutes later the car pulled to a halt in the Footscray Primary School car park, where we waited outside the playground with all the other Teochew families for our tour bus to arrive. The Teochew Chinese Friendship Association consisted mostly of old folk who liked to sit in buses and look out the windows, plus a smattering of families with children. The adults were responsible for hiring the bus, while the elderly were responsible for the entertainment – namely, singing and clapping and carrying a tune down ten different paths that rarely converged. Sometimes my uncle liked to bring his mandolin, to lend a twanging unity to the Sino Sunrise Singers. That was the name I gave our choir, because their music could wake anybody up.

'Did you know,' my father asked as we passed a farm with a 'Trespassers Will Be Prosecuted' sign out the front, 'that if you enter someone else's farm property they can shoot you?' He was sitting next to me with his face pressed against the window, absorbing the largeness of the Victorian landscape.

I wondered whether he knew the difference between the words 'prosecuted' and 'persecuted'. It probably made no difference in his mind, having come from a country where people gave way to cars, and landmines gave way to no one.

'Look at the Australian country kids,' my mother marvelled as we passed a group of tweens at a rural bus stop, dressed in Target couture. 'So sophisticated.' She was comparing them to the country kids she knew in Cambodia who, as labourers on the land, were a different breed from the city folk. When they first arrived at the Melbourne Midway Migrant Hostel, these country Cambodians, including my parents, were scared of escalators and cars, the latter for good reason – in Cambodia, cars were random curses that ran down families. But they liked elevators. Without words to discriminate between experiences, a ride in an elevator with a window was just as good as a ride at Luna Park. For my parents it was actually better, because it was free.

When our bus arrived at the strawberry farm, some of the oldies decided to stay on board and sleep. We younger ones lined up and paid our $6 entry fee to the young woman standing at the gate, her brown ponytail pulled so tight we were surprised her ears didn't meet at the back of her head when she turned around. My father looked bewildered as a white two-litre ice-cream container was placed in his hands. 'You carry the fruit in these,' advised the woman, 'and I will now take you to the picking fields. Please stay within the first two fields. Do not venture off into the other fields.'

'At the cherry farm we got buckets,' my mother muttered in Teochew. We were led past fields filled with lush red fruits dripping with gorgeousness. The Teochew crew 'wahhhed' over each strawberry we passed, pointing here, there and everywhere.

Finally the brown-haired woman stopped. 'These are the picking fields,' she said, then left. We stood there, searching for strawberries, and realised that the ground had been so picked over there was barely any fruit to be seen. I wondered if everyone else felt gypped too.

'Did you know that my first job in the Aussie countryside was fruit picking?' my father mentioned as we searched for stray strawberries. 'All the migrants of the Midway Migrant Hostel left on a bus very early in the morning, and we came back late in the evening.'

As the field gradually filled with more people, we realised that all the other visitors, in their Colorado jeans and their Billabong bumbags, had not been led to the picking area. They had just walked here. And they had buckets. Big yellow buckets swung from their hands. Even the children had them. I pretended I hadn't noticed, but my little sister Alina piped up, 'Hey, Alice, how come they got buckets?' I glanced at my father and saw that he had noticed too. I watched him watch the old Teochew men and women, clutching each other and their little ice-cream containers, spluttering with mirth at the fact they were now paying to do labour they had been paid to do when they first arrived in Australia.

'Hey, Alice,' whined Alina, who always wanted answers to questions, 'why did we get ice-cream containers?' A dozen other little eyes also looked at me, laden with expectation. I stared at my container for a while and then explained to our little siblings and cousins that it was purely for aesthetic reasons that the yellow people were given white ice-cream cartons, while the white people were given yellow buckets. Although we couldn't swing our ice-cream cartons like buckets, I demonstrated how they made good helmets for our heads.

My mother and my auntie came bounding up. 'Look what we have!' They thrust their containers in our faces.

I couldn't believe what I saw. 'Where did you get those?'

'They're huge!' breathed my sister Alison.

'Over there,' pointed my mother.

The unauthorised field. They had been picking in the unauthorised field. My mother hadn't understood the English admonitions at the start, and she was miffed at the small ice-cream containers we had been given. During the Pol Pot years they had become used to going into one another's abandoned houses. It was a free-for-all then, and she had probably chosen to believe that it still was.

We brought this on ourselves, really, my father was probably thinking as he looked at his container filled with its small tokens of compliance. He didn't kick up a fuss or demand to know why we were given containers one-third the size of the others', because we didn't want to hear from them what we already knew. It seemed that the other visitors didn't have *kiasu* bad habits like we did: the kind of habit that made you cling to fear like there was no tomorrow.

The others would never pick the forbidden fruit. They didn't pull strawberries like madcap machines and then stand in a corner chucking the slightly bruised ones to the ground. We were not known for casually strolling and picking and enjoying the scenery. We pounced on each berry like overexcited labradors, and we picked like labourers.

'Look at this one shaped like a house,' announced my sister Alison.

'Stop wasting time,' said my mother, 'and find some good ones.' Her carton was filled with even more big red stunners, and she had stayed within the boundaries this time. She wouldn't eat the strawberries, or let us eat them, until they had been washed. 'Aiyah, you don't want to die!'

My auntie was ecstatic when she found a tap. 'Ay, come here! Wash them here!' she called as she held the container under the torrential tap.

'Please don't use the rainwater to wash the berries,' the farm's owner said as he walked past.

'But those ghosts were doing it,' my aunt muttered to my father. True, but the Anglo-Australians weren't turning on the taps full-throttle. My auntie had not realised that there were water restrictions now; she still believed that the water Down Under, like everything else in this wondrous world, would never run out.

When the berries were washed, we unpacked our picnic. 'Where is the stale bread?' asked my uncle. 'There are birds here to feed.'

When my family first arrived in Malcolm Fraser's Australia, the sign of a great democracy was being able to feed stale bread to the seagulls, and they had been doing it ever since.

The pork roll was cut, the fresh bread retrieved, and the Lo Han Guo passed around and around in its never-ending flask. It was a good day of labour, and 10,000 photographs were taken just in case anyone ever needed a flick-animation book of the event. We were tired and sticky, and clambered back on the bus with our berries in plastic bags. Some of the children were so tired they even managed to sleep through my uncle strumming Chinese lullabies and communist folk songs on his mandolin.

My mother scrabbled around in our picnic box, trying to find a space for the strawberries. She pulled out a box of chocolates she had been saving for a family trip. It was slightly past its use-by date because she had kept it for so long. 'Hah!' she cried. 'Look at this!' She held a sweet up to the sinking sunlight. She told us that each strawberry we picked had cost as much as a Ferrero Rocher chocolate, and that next time we should just go to Big W to buy lollies instead. It would save time and petrol and effort. But I could tell she did not regret this day, that it was a fulfilling one of good and meaningful work, because the chocolates were shared around and eaten, while the strawberries were still saved in the picnic box, to be taken home.

HOLIDAY AT
SLACKS CREEK

I liked the sound of Slacks Creek. It sounded like a place where people wore badly fitting trousers and loitered about doing sweet bugger-all. But as soon as I saw Mum pack the frypan, the pot, the icebox and the Pine-O Cleen into our suitcase, I knew there was no chance of us doing that on our first Australian family holiday.

'Expect the houses to look like the ones in Braybrook, but on stilts,' warned my mum when we were on the plane. We had grown up in Braybrook, Victoria, a town filled with the noxious fumes of carpet factories. Once, Dad and I had seen a picture of our former prime minister's childhood home in a newspaper. It looked just like ours – white and square – and we had suddenly felt an affinity with our leader. Now we were going to holiday in a Paul Keating–childhood commission home on legs. My father was as excited as a pioneer about this Queensland trip. 'The real estate agent connected up the electricity and water for us, so everything is all set to go!'

My parents had bought this house, inspired by our Aunt May. My aunt had secured herself a whole string of Queensland proper-ties, and spent summer holidays fixing them up. My uncle and aunt would drive their family of young kids up from Melbourne with a carload of crockery and dried Asian food, and sometimes even a second-hand television. They stayed in their unrentable ramshackle houses, and my very handy uncle would change the carpets, fix the lights and paint the walls until the property was in top shape again. Then they'd rent it out and move on to do the next one.

They were resourceful and hard-working and good-humoured, but of course we could never ask them to have a look at our investment property in Slacks Creek. It was like a phlegmy sick relative with rotting teeth no one wanted to go near. Every time a new injury was discovered – faulty stove, dodgy cupboards that would not close, a slightly shifty wall – the real estate agent would call us up in Melbourne. A while after the last tenants left, and I asked my dad what we should do, because the house had already not been rented out for five weeks.

'Don't worry,' he said. 'It's about time we took a family holiday. Then we'll get it fixed up.'

But when we arrived in Queensland, I realised that people did not take their holidays in Slacks Creek. I realised this when I saw the house next to ours. It had four and a half cars parked out the front, with grass growing between some of the wheels. A father and his scruffy-haired child came out and watched Dad back the car into our driveway. I watched the bewilderment on our new neighbour's face when he noticed the Europcar sticker on the windscreen. *What the fig? What kind of neighbour hires a silver Tarago?*

We got out, and looked up at the three-bedroom, unrenovated Queenslander that had been rejected by three tenants. 'The houses in the Cambodian countryside were built like this,' my father told us, 'and they kept buffaloes below.' We had never seen a Queenslander before. We marvelled at the wooden beams beneath the house, while my mother beamed because she had four kids and did not need to pay for a hotel. This would be our home for the next ten days. This was awesome. As we helped Mum unload supplies from the car, my brother and I secretly felt like refugees for the first time in our lives.

We drove to Woolworths and bought a week's worth of food, a mop and spider-killer spray. When we returned we tied Chux wipes to our feet and skidded along the floorboards in the living room. My sister Alina crawled around like a labrador, with cleaning cloths on her hands and knees. My brother, Alexander, wiped the windows with Windex. He looked out. 'The neighbours are still watching us.'

'Don't worry,' said my dad. 'We just look like a hard-working migrant family.'

He had said a similar thing when someone once chucked a stone through our front window in Braybrook. It left a large crack and we didn't get it repaired until we sold the house. 'Don't worry. We're just living humbly,' he would say. We never opened that window again, and kept the blinds drawn. Bit by bit, the house of my childhood grew darker as the trees grew larger outside with no one to prune them. 'Don't worry. We're just living privately,' said my dad.

But before we were completely closed in by all this private humility, and to get away from the carpet factory fumes, we moved. My parents had worked for two decades to buy our booming birthday-cake of a mansion on the hill. After we moved, we lost our asthma and gained a greater appreciation for the genteel lifestyle of our new prime minister in Kirribilli House. My mother also discovered White King, the household bleach that could disinfect anything.

She had brought the White King to Slacks Creek. She rolled up her trousers and scrubbed the bathtub, because it would also become our laundry basin for the holiday. There were no beds but we had enough sleeping bags and blankets to spread out on the floor of the living room. We all lay on the floorboards that first night, happy and exhausted. The warmth of the Queensland evening felt good.

'Haven't been this way for ages,' said Dad.

'What way?' asked Mum.

'The sleeping-on-the-floor way.'

My parents had walked across Cambodia, Vietnam and Thailand before they were accepted to come to Australia. They had slept on many floors. 'It's nice to get back to one's refugee roots,' sighed Dad.

'Make sure those roots don't get head lice,' warned my mother.

'Mum, we haven't had head lice for years,' I protested. 'Those sleeping bags are clean.'

'When we were in the Thai refugee camp,' Dad continued, 'we slept on a straw mat about this size.' He indicated an area the size of one of our sleeping bags. 'That was a very good and productive mat,' he said. 'You were manufactured on that mat. Manufactured in Thailand, but assembled in Australia.'

'Ewww!' I said, but my father liked telling that story about how I came to be.

'Ewww!' my brother said.

*

The next morning, we woke up early to begin our drive to the first theme park: Movie World. Mum was already up. She had washed and hung out our clothes from yesterday's cleaning spree and was now rummaging through our supplies of food in the icebox. 'Cockroaches!' she screamed.

'Just whack it with your shoe,' said Dad. We hadn't seen one of those for years, because of Mum's White King. 'Where did we put the bacon we bought last night for breakfast?'

Coming from years of war and starvation, my family were parsimonious with everything except food: we ate lychees and abalone, prawns and mangoes in our house. My siblings and I couldn't say 'we're starving' to parents who knew what it was like to starve. We couldn't say 'I'm dying of boredom' to parents who knew what death in decomposing multitudes was like. So we could never really be hungry or bored on holidays.

Every day Dad would drive us out to do the usual things holidaying families did in Queensland. We visited the Big Pineapple and the Sunshine Coast. My brother bought my sister a furry white toy seal at Sea World, and we had our pictures taken at Wet'n'Wild, howling down a waterslide on a floaty round raft. But we'd return to the house in Slacks Creek every evening, where local children walked barefoot to the Woolworths with a fistful of coins and bought icy poles. We'd sit on the verandah after Mum had made dinner and spray on the Aerogard.

We were lucky that we were not refugees and that this was all a game, a game paid for by our parents. Dad did not gather us round, wave his arm over our property in Slacks Creek and say: 'Someday, this mortgage will all be yours,' but we knew. One evening Mum said: 'Someday you will all have families and you will take them on holidays like this one.' But I also knew that we would probably never take our families on such trips. We were not really brave like our parents. We would just book hotels, because we would never be as resourceful and self-sacrificial to the next generation. Dad and Mum had arrived in Australia with one suitcase, and there was nothing in it. This probably explained why they packed so much on holidays.

On the last day, Dad called the real estate agent to arrange for repairs to the house. Mum told me to pop over to the neighbours and give them our remaining theme park tickets. As we loaded our frypans and cleaning supplies into the back of the rented silver Tarago, the neighbour and his daughter stood outside watching us, the Sea World tickets still in their hands. We must have been the weirdest tenants they'd ever met.

We waved to them as we drove off, and they waved back.

'We're all going on a summer holiday!' Tony Tran was singing again, with a chorus of bikini-clad girls swinging in the background. There were about 120 of these girls, because he was standing in front of thirty TV sets at my family's Retravision store in Footscray, and all the tellies were linked up to the same budget beach-scenes karaoke DVD. Tony's sweeping arm actions brought out the best in his bling microfibre shirt. He often wore these shirts in substitute for our standard blue sales uniform. 'No more working for a week or two,' he crooned. Customers stopped to watch and applaud him. Salesmen stopped to watch the girls on the telly. And I stopped to adjust a store sign that was peeling from the heat.

We put signs up declaring the holiday season, but in our world, there were only three seasons: pre-sale, sale and stocktake. It was a Saturday afternoon in the middle of a Melbourne summer, and while our Australian customers were backpacking around China, I was busy unpacking boxes of cassette tapes made in China. Our less worldly friends spent their school breaks home-bound with their rear-projection TVs and icemaker fridges, their safe white-bread sandwiches. But there were dangers, our parents believed, for those poor kids alone in those massive suburban mansions. They would want to use the stove without adult supervision, and their pikelet dreams would turn into inextinguishable house-fire nightmares. There was nothing like the safety of the store.

During 30-degree days, my father set up his own demonstration outside the store to sell ice-shavers. We filled polystyrene cups with shaved ice, added a dash of cordial, and the dehydrated world hurrying past stopped to smile at us. This was like a lemonade stand, but better – we weren't kids fundraising for new rollerskates, we were workers helping with serious business. As we grew older, we became sales assistants with our own name tags, our personalities pared down to one pithy, perked-up line: 'How can I help you?'

'Excuse me.'

I looked up from the half-sliced box of cassettes and saw a small Asian woman with a smile like a slice of watermelon. 'Microwave broken.'

All customers around this neighbourhood communicated with an essential efficiency – almost no words and all action.

The lady pointed to a receipt in her hand. 'I want buy new microwave.' She pointed to the model number on her receipt. 'Same that one.'

'But your microwave's still under warranty,' I told her. 'We can fix it – for free.'

'No good have anything broken for the New Year,' she told me. 'Bring bad luck.'

During the time before Chinese and Vietnamese New Year in late February, customers often bought new water urns, kettles and rice cookers, even if their old ones were still under warranty. My mother told me that back in Cambodia, during New Year, the whole community stopped working to visit each other. They were the happiest times of her life, she said, because she would get a new set of clothes every year. But when your family owns an electrical appliance store that operates seven days a week, the only way you notice the arrival of Chinese New Year is in the increase of white-goods purchases.

You know Christmas has come when the Sunbeam Corporation sends a gigantic white bear in a beanie and scarf, to be raffled off to customers. And you can tell summer has arrived not from the vision of heat outside, but by the box of bright Hawaiian shirts sent by Retravision head office for our summer promotional uniform.

Working hours were not kind to cultural celebrations, particularly when we were competing with the hi-fi megastore down the road. But at least we still got new clothes, even if the shipment didn't always arrive in time and Tony Tran had to improvise with his own glossy attire.

During the school holidays, our family spent quality time working together, surrounded by an eccentric everyday cast of hundreds. There was a man with a watering can who went around watering the money trees near the front doors of the stores so that the businesses would thrive. We always gave him a tip. There was also a carpet-cleaner salesman who scrubbed his detergents on shop carpets in strategic places. If the store owners didn't buy the cleaning liquids, they'd be left bewildered at the huge smiley face scrubbed into their carpets, showing up the years of grime.

Unlike a conventional electrical-goods franchise, we also sold appliances that distinctively appealed to the Asian diaspora: Tiger rice cookers, deluxe 'Rolls Royce' automated toilets and electronic English–Vietnamese dictionaries. In fact, there were so many little things to buy in this town that, as children, we rarely even thought of wanting bigger things. After school, instead of coming back to watch one TV, we'd watch twenty in a row, and sometimes be joined by the children of customers, who'd squeal when they were dragged away by one arm from *Captain Planet.*

'Everybody has a summer holiday, doing things they always wanted to!'

Tony Tran was in such a good mood because that morning we'd been visited by the Chinese New Year Dragon. Puppeteered by four young men from the local dance troupe, its arrival through the shopping strip was heralded by drums, cymbals and fire-crackers. Most of the migrant inhabitants of this neighbourhood had escaped from some war or another, so you might think they'd hide with hands over their ears when they heard the racket. But no, they wanted small business to be blessed with prosperity by a creature whose arrival was hailed by a series of machine-gun sounds. The exploding noise of the firecrackers would scare away evil spirits, and the staff sought out the mouth of the dragon to slip in lucky red envelopes of money: an innocuous bribe against the sway of the superstores.

'No, sorry mate, unfortunately the karaoke DVDs are not included,' Tony Tran said, as he carried the DVD player he'd sold to the register. His customer asked him something else. 'No, sorry mate, I can't burn you a copy here either. How about I give you a New Year's present? How about this t-shirt?'

The customer seemed quite pleased with his Electronic Soya-Milk Maker t-shirt.

Once a year, right in the middle of summer, when other Australians were at the beach getting tanned, the carnival material-ised right in front of our shop. Whole streets were blocked off in the Footscray central business district and Luna Park came to us, complete with the upside-down machines and spinning teacups. Retailers would set up small tents to advertise their stores or sell

Vietnamese CDs; street vendors would grind sugarcane to sell as drinks, or roast pork balls and corn.

My father promoted mobile phone deals in a little hired tent down the street, my aunties and I staffed the shop, and an assortment of small cousins and siblings would loiter about waiting for us to finish work and take them to the revelry.

We finally closed shop and stepped outside. A different world emerged, populated by brown and yellow faces in wide-brimmed hats to ensure that no tan would reach South-East Asian skin. (For the older women, the anaemic aristocrat look was always the fashion.) Our mayor made the usual speech about multiculturalism that no one under the age of twenty-five listened to because they were too excited waiting to see the local South-East Asian version of the Backstreet Boys.

These boys were good, and what was even better was that they often crooned Carpenters hits. They dressed in matching polyester shirts and sang about being on top of the world. We passed Tony Tran in the audience, getting ready to groove, with a skewer of barbequed octopus in one hand.

People gave him a wide berth.

We passed my father in his tent, packing up brochures. He handed us a roll of tickets to the rides.

'Use all these up tonight,' he instructed. The rides had come into our town from the Springvale festival, and next weekend the New Year's celebrations would move to Richmond. As I sat with my sisters on the ferris wheel over Footscray, I looked down to my world peopled with colour and realised there was no need to paint this neighbourhood red. Firecrackers in the morning, a dragon through the store in the afternoon and a carnival in the evening – you could live your whole life in a town, but your world would still be filled with small wonders.

VISITS

CAVEAT EMPTOR

There are two important things your Chinese parents will teach you in life. First, don't owe any debts; and second, own your own property. Unlike their other attempts at edification, these two lessons are non-gender-specific. A year or so after you have started full-time work, after you've paid off your university loan in one lump sum, your parents will begin to bug you about buying a house. Your mother and father will insist that you get the property in *your own name*, in case you marry a man who might want to leave you, gamble or steal your assets – or, worse, a white ghost who *does not want to share*. In twenty-five years of marriage, your father has given every cent he has earned to your mother.

Your father will spend a day each weekend with you – a day where he could be working at his store – looking at houses. In the car, driving from property to property, you will have conversations about many things. Your father will tell you about the importance of owning an investment property, explain the concept of negative gearing, and discuss family trusts and tax offsets. But most importantly he will teach you, indirectly, about security and the importance of saving.

When your mother was younger, she worked in a factory and saved all her earnings in a jar stashed underneath her pillow.

When your great-grandmother died, the family couldn't afford a funeral because they had spent all their savings on her week in hospital. Fortunately, your mother had that jar beneath her pillow.

In Pol Pot's Cambodia, your father once took the belt from his waist and buried it where no one would find it. He then watched as the people around him died of starvation. He was responsible for burying their bodies on higher ground when the floods came, so that their corpses would not contaminate the Mekong River. One day, when he felt as if soon he too might be one of those bodies, he dug up the belt, cut it into small strips and boiled it for hours in secret. Then he called his mother and sister over, and they ate it. In this way, they stayed alive.

Your father will tell you that you don't want to live a life of in-the-moment hedonism like a lot of Australians, always spending what they have and often what they don't have. But you know he's not talking about credit-card debt or mortgages. This is what you have inherited: this knowledge that to save your family you have to save things. And that is why the idea of the investment property looms so large in the migrant version of the Great Australian Dream. It secures your existence.

The areas your father targets are the western suburbs of Melbourne, from which you came: the properties in front of the carpet factory in Braybrook; the weatherboard homes in Footscray, Sunshine and Maidstone. You plan your day according to open-house times, and park the car five minutes before the agent arrives. Already there is a line forming outside. At every house you inspect there are at least five other Asian couples or families. You can't tell which are planning to buy investment properties and which are wanting to break the rental cycle, as you are all dressed in shabby Saturday clothes that you have owned for decades or made yourselves.

When you enter, you are hit by a familiar scent, an icky mix of nostalgia and stuffy nausea. In these small homes the smells of sleep, cooking and daily life permeate every crevice. You see the sewing machine next to the baby's cot in the back room, the Laminex and cork tables, the curtains nearly falling off their hinges but always drawn so outsiders can't look inside and see the Asians engaging in tax-evasive work. You see the children's rooms, with none of the pink-and-blue-and-laden-with-toys look of Target ads, but packed with boxes filled with miscellany from import businesses, or stacks of cut fabric pieces. You look down and see the grouting of the tiles clotted with blackness. You look up and see the plastic prints of fluorescent deities on the wall – Buddha or Jesus looking down on you, condemning your condescension. You go outside to backyards filled with weeds and broken clotheslines.

Your father does not seem to be affected by all this. 'How many square metres is it? What is the rental in the area like?' he asks the agent, and takes down notes.

'Of course you're not going to live in it,' your father says when you voice your dismay at how certain properties are falling apart, how the wooden beams have been eaten away by rot, how window-sills are cracking. They are investment properties to him, but walking around inside you see that they are real residences inhabited by people leading temporary, rented lives – waiting, waiting to make it, all the while working in the grot and gritty stickiness.

One time, you and your father venture to Carlton, to see an old terrace house that has been advertised for a steal. You think about this house, and about what it would be like to own and *live* in your own home so close to the city. When you walk through it you know that you would not just be investing in an asset but in cultural capital, the chance for a very different life.

When your father walks inside and sees the renovations, he thinks about the exorbitant rental prices in Carlton. He is thrilled for you. He tells you to check the contract of sale on the table while he inspects the new extensions – extensions that are not approved by the building council, as you soon discover in the vendor's statement. Approval for a permit is conditional on 'restoring the house back to its natural fittings and rooms to their original use': the extended rumpus room has to be knocked down, the original positioning of windows reinstated. The kitchen that has been turned into a washing room has to be turned back into a kitchen. The real-estate agent standing outside never murmurs a word about this to anyone. He is under no obligation to, because in this area of law it's *caveat emptor*.

The white couples walking though the house talk excitedly about attending the auction next week. Many of them don't even bother to look at the contract, so taken in are they by the low asking price.

You motion your dad over and explain what you have discovered. You're both flabbergasted: there are around two pages of unauthorised renovations. Alarmed, you both decide to leave. As you walk down the steps of the porch, your father unexpectedly meets a Chinese friend.

'Ay, boss,' your father warns, 'be very careful about this house.'

'Hah? Why?'

'Do you know why it's so cheap?'

'Because it's half-finished,' says the friend, 'but no worries. I can fix the rest of it myself. It's a good investment, eh?'

Your father explains about the unauthorised extensions and the building permit. You watch the realisation dawn on the man's face. 'Thank you for telling me this, boss,' he tells your father. 'I can't read the contract, so I would have come to the auction and bid.'

'No worries, mate,' says your father. 'My daughter's a lawyer, so lucky for us she can spot these things.'

The next stop is an auction in Footscray. The street is packed with lines of cars and people, almost as if for a school fête. Bidding has started, and already you see Asian people walking away from the property. 'Forget it, boss,' says a man in Vietnamese as he moves off slowly in his four-wheel drive, 'it's already over $410,000.'

But you both stay for the auction, and by the end of it you both can't believe that a dilapidated little house in Macpherson Street could go for almost half a million dollars. It is the very house that your parents first rented when they got here, the house you were brought home to from the hospital. But this is Footscray, after all, a suburb not immune to gentrification. It appears that you might never be able to afford your first home in this area, but sometimes it is good to move on.

OPPORTUNITY

There is a severed bear's head in the hall, and it has been there for more than a week. Its red tongue pokes out from its mouth, which is caught in a bewildered beam. The bear's body lies elsewhere, in another room. It does not smell, although foamy polyester threads poke out of its neck like petrified silkworms. Its eyes are glassy and scratched. Next to the head is a blue dress with its arms cut off. Some plastic beads lie there, the type that would be hazardous if inhaled up a baby's nostril.

When the students have a dress-up party, they take the tram up Sydney Road, Brunswick, to a second-hand megastore called Savers. They come back with bridesmaids' dresses, handmade by someone's aunt, and hack them short for an '80s party. The blue frock is for a retro night. The head is ripped off the enormous soft teddy to use as a mask in an outfit for a superheroes party. The red shirt is for a Rubik's Cube party, where each person dresses in colours and swaps items of clothing through the evening, until they meander home at 2 am, exult-ant in borrowed monochrome. Graham Greene wrote a short story, 'The Destructors', about boys who dismantle an old man's house bit by bit. But this is not careful destruction; this seems like tearing out the foundations. Holes are gouged into stockings from another era. Cameo pins are pricked into an old man's softly brushed waistcoat.

'You look awesome!'

'You also look great!'

High-fives all round as the students roll out the door.

In another suburb, a man without words tries on a pair of trousers, a lined jacket and a similar waistcoat. He sees that the latter was tailor-made in Italy, with craftsmanship rarely seen these days. It is a good fit, but he stands still, too embarrassed to approach the woman behind the counter.

'What can I do for you?' she asks, smiling. The man knows she has seen him, that now he must step forward. He looks down at the glass counter, beneath which lies the more expensive jewellery items and hand-painted plates.

'You have come on a lucky day,' she tells him as she takes the three-piece suit. 'Today is half-price day.' With the discount, the clothes come to a total of $5.40. The man counts out his coins. He stays silent because they do not speak the same language. The woman notices that the man is 30 cents short, but does not say anything. She gives him back his 50-cent coin in change. He too does not say anything, but slides it back towards her. She insists: 'Half-price day!' She is confusing him, so he takes the money.

In America they are called thrift stores, which makes them sound like places for stingy hoarders; but here they are op-shops, real places of opportunity, so much so that two artists and Victoria University lecturers, Sue Dodd and Enza Gandolfo, decided to write a book called *Inventory* and create an art exhibition using only donated items from op-shops. At the launch I meet 84-year-old Elsie Seidel-Davis, who has been volunteering at the West Footscray Uniting Church's op-shop for sixteen years. Without the op-shop, she says, she wouldn't know what to do with herself. Her friends agree. They tell me that people working in such places are never just sales assistants; they become counsellors, social workers, administrators.

Elsie points to the videos on display, which show women in the back rooms of op-shops sorting out donated goods. Tonnes of stretchy, twice-worn Supré clothes are donated every month, but only 30 per cent of all donations actually make it to the shops; the rest are shipped overseas. This culling means that the poor here can have good things. But the only people who seem to use that word publicly these days – 'poor' – are the Brotherhood of St Laurence and university students. Some students use it after coming back from a year of travelling around the world. 'I'm so poor,' they say, 'but at least I gained my independence!'

In the places they travelled, they could, if they wanted, see the origins of their clothes. In China, silk cloth has been made since the Shang era (1600 BC), and cotton since the Song Dynasty (960–1279). Men picked the cotton and farmed the silkworms, and women wove the cloth. Making a gown was a noble trade back then, or at least that is the way it appears in the museums displaying ancient handicrafts. But often, the marvels of modern manufacturing remain obscure – after all, a student on a self-discovery tour probably does not want to visit a factory where shorts are being sewn. It's easier to have a neat political statement about the marginalisation of third-world workers printed on a t-shirt. Half the things we wear in Australia, in any case, already come with a prêt-à-porter, socio-economic-political label: Made in China. And because it's all so cheap, we have more outfits to stuff into the orange donation bags left in our letterboxes than ever before – and most of it ends up getting sent back overseas.

When my parents first arrived in Australia, they were given a bag of baby clothes from the Brotherhood of St Laurence. My mother took the clothes to the laundromat to wash them, and when she returned she found that someone had emptied out her machine and stolen them all. Since then, my father has travelled the world and returned with impressive Italian dresses for her, but she still mentions that bag of clothes. (My friend Khoa once told me that his mum was also given a bag of baby clothes, and when she opened the bag she realised they were for girls. So he and his brother wore frocks for the first years of their lives.) As a migrant, there is nothing like having the skin of your most precious possession touched by the grace of charity. I understand something of why my mother laments those baby clothes: having a gift pinched is different from someone stealing something you bought and can buy again. And it is difficult to buy such quality in shops these days. You either have to go to boutiques, or visit an op-shop.

In the morning, the aftermath of the students' revelry is strewn about the hall again: discarded garments sticky with Bacardi Breezer, cheap beer and occasional traces of vomit and other bodily effluence – signifiers of living an independent life at eighteen, debris to be cleaned up later.

For Elsie, though, independence is straightening the bows on brown bears with pokey-tongued smiles, and selling suits on half-price day. And for the man walking out of the store, it's a plastic bag containing clothes that will make him a new man in a new country.

SILENCE OF THE PHONES

Dharma Drum Mountain Buddhist Chan (Zen)
Meditation Centre in Templestowe

'If you tell your leg to stop hurting,' says the Venerable Monk, 'does it listen to you?' We're not meant to look at him when he's speaking. We have to focus on our sitting, because he's walking around with the incense board in his hand. The incense board is like a flat whacking-stick, to be used if any of us nods off during meditation. When it's swung against someone's back, it makes a noise that jolts the rest upright.

'The triangle is the most stable shape in trigonometry,' the Venerable explains, 'so that's why we sit in full lotus.' The full-lotus position is sitting cross-legged, with your left foot on your right thigh and your right foot on your left thigh. It locks you in, so you can focus on training your mind while sitting in the semi-dark facing a blank wall in the Buddhist Meditation Centre.

Chan Buddhism, which the Japanese call Zen, was introduced to China from India by a monk named Boddhidharma. It is said that Boddhidharma sat in a cave for nine years before he attained enlightenment. They say he sat so still for so long that his shadow became permanently etched on the wall.

When we enter the meditation hall, we must leave all our distractions outside. The monk passes around a basket for us to deliver over our final attachment to the outside world. Everyone looks anxiously at the stack of mobile phones as they drop theirs in, but no one says a word, because this is a five-day silent retreat. There is also to be no reading or writing, or tactile contact with anyone.

According to the most recent census, Buddhism is the fastest growing religion in Australia. We have the earthly signifiers to prove it – the biggest Buddhist temple in the southern hemisphere is the Nan Tien, or 'Paradise of the South', a Fo Guang Shan temple near Port Kembla. There are massive stupas in unassuming suburbs, as well as small temples and meditation centres dotted all over the land, for different denominations: Mahayanan, Theravadan, Tibetan, Sri Lankan, Pure Land, Thai Forest Tradition, Zen or Chan. But it's the heart of the practice, not these buildings, that matters, all the Venerables say. During my first retreat, a friend who almost became a monk explained Chan Buddhism to me: 'It's like having a single flower in an empty room. Some people don't see the point of the empty room, but it's the empty room that brings out the beauty of the flower.'

Quite a few Buddhist centres conduct retreats. It is here that people learn fast that the festively plump Buddha in their backyard water feature may be rollicking in fits of laughter, but the actual practice is very painful. If it isn't, then we're taking shortcuts. No pain, no gain. Even without any distractions, I find I can't sit still for half an hour without suffering. The side of my ear itches. Unexpected spasms shoot through my leg. The backside is more complicated than I'd appreciated: every time there is a clenching ache, I discover a new muscle. Out of the corner of my eye I notice 65-year-old Irene, who has sat still for an hour, unperturbed by my restless shifting.

I also discover how quickly feelings of loving-kindness cultivated in the last half-hour dissipate when the person next to me releases gas. Because we are not supposed to move, all our attention is focused inwards – and we start to magnify all our small irritations. What a torment the mind is.

Mine starts thinking about mobile phones a lot, because I have just relinquished mine, and also because it used to be my job to sell them. In the silence, I realise that I was a speech peddler – that when I sold a phone, I was helping people to discharge their verbal effluent at the cheapest cost. In the past, only schizophrenics or sages heard a thousand voices in their heads. Now, anyone who doesn't hear these voices is seen to be cutting themselves off from society. A person's phone is like a lively child they can show off to others: *Look! Mine can sing, vibrate to a tune, show faces, play games and remember important events.* But after the sound-and-light show, it is dumped in the bottom of a handbag clotted with congealed lollies and used bus tickets. It is suddenly bewildering to me how a whole living person can be compacted to this small plastic rectangle. I marvel that we don't have more reverence for the device, because it would have been a miracle to a person living two centuries ago. The quiet also reminds me that there used to be a time when people saved their speech for certain periods, a time when words had more weight.

After a few days, I begin to do things without so much witless white-noise commentary in my mind. Our heads, hands, ears and eyes are kept busy in other ways. The gong wakes us up at 4.30 in the morning, while it is still dark, to do yoga exercises so our muscles don't cramp up. Between silent sittings, we sweep and mop and clean. We eat our meals in silence, so we can reflect on all the efforts of the thousands of sentient beings it took for a single grain of rice to reach our bowls: from the first person, who planted the rice seeds, to the last, who scooped it into the dish.

After eating, we rinse our bowls with hot water and drink up the residue, so nothing is wasted. We wash up. The Venerable then fills each of our bowls almost to the brim with water, and directs us to walk around the great perimeter of the centre without spilling a single drop. It takes me three attempts to understand how much effort it takes to be careful. Then we go back to our sitting.

My fellow retreat-goers are not people with lots of time on their hands. They are Chinese parents and professionals and other full-time workers who have saved up their annual leave to do this. In theory, it's about being present in all our thoughts and actions. In practice, it's about learning to sleep through the night when a stranger in the bunk below is snoring heavily from a cold. It's about quietening your mind down enough that you are no longer affected by severe, irrational annoyance, and about recognising that a noise is just a noise. And if sleeping through the night is impossible, then it's about not whingeing in the morning.

When the retreat ends, we are allowed to talk again and our mobile phones are handed back. There is a world outside to catch up with, because we've slowed down so much. Some people switch their phones back on when they get into their cars. Others put theirs back in their bags and still don't speak. We've only just begun to realise what silly, monomaniacal obsessions we think and talk about each day, so we make resolutions to listen. We leave the Chan hall and the door closes, with its sign intact: 'Noble silence please'.

SCREEN DUMPS

'I met this guy,' Bianca told Ally late one night as she was driv-ing. They always talked in Bianca's car when it was on the move. 'I've been chatting to him for a while now. He's really keen on me,' she said.

'What's his name?' Ally asked.

'Mike. He's pretty serious about me.' She mentioned how Mike had an American accent and what a turn-on that was for her.

The summer before she met Bianca, Ally and her cousins caught flies in plastic bags. Once they caught forty-seven in an afternoon, and tied the bag up. When the early-evening winds were blowing, they let the bag go up with the breeze. They watched it for a while, and then went back inside. Then one day Bianca showed up on her doorstep. She was the only one from primary school who kept coming back.

It was strange – despite how long they'd been together, their pri-vate griefs had never been shared: the death of Ally's grandmother, the death of Bianca's pets. And until recently, the ending of their romantic relationships. *Grieving is like falling in love backwards,* wrote an American poet who also happened to be an undertaker. Falling in love, for the both of them, was a very private matter. Then one day – they had no idea how it came about – they grew up.

They were no longer living with their parents, but still within fifteen kilometres of each other. Bianca would pick Ally up in her car and take her on long drives to the 24-hour Kmart.

A week later, Bianca told Ally about her first date with Mike. They had watched a movie together. She showed Ally a picture of herself from that evening. Her face was aglow, not from special lighting, but from the presence of the person at the other end of the camera. Bianca and Mike could not kiss, but they soon began to see each other every day. They left each other messages on their mobile phones. 'He sings songs to me while I get ready for work,' Bianca said. 'I wake up to him in the morning saying, "Good morning, baby, time to get up."'

Bianca showed Ally a photo of him on her mobile phone. He was a young man with a smile and a goatee.

After a couple of weeks, Bianca told Ally that Mike wanted to meet her. Bianca asked her to come over after work. First Bianca drove her to Coles to buy some frozen dinners. 'Don't worry, he'll be there waiting for me when I get home. He always is.'

They went upstairs to Bianca's room. Bianca turned on the computer. 'Hello, Mike,' Ally said, waving at the screen.

It must have been very early in the morning for him in the States. He had put on a white shirt with blue hatches. 'Hi.' He gave her a little wave.

'How's life in Alabama?'

'Not bad. Not bad. I'm doin' alright.'

They chatted effortlessly and even joked around a bit. Somehow, he seemed more real and three-dimensional than some men Ally had dated, who would sit opposite her at a table in a restaurant and deliver a tally of all their successes, and measure the weight of her worth like human calculators.

Hooking up their computer cameras, Bianca and Mike had

more movie dates. They would turn on their televisions and DVD players and put on the same film to watch at exactly the same time. The computer camera was always positioned at an angle so that the eyes appeared large and luminous in the head, and the chin smaller. Bianca's lamp was carefully positioned so as to give off a nice glow. Bianca taught Ally all about screen dumps, which was taking a still picture of someone while they were on camera, but which sounded to Ally like taking a crap or breaking up. Of course she never told Bianca this. She did not want to jinx their burgeoning relationship.

Bianca and Mike did the things that normal couples do. He slept with her, in that he would go to sleep on webcam, and so would she, and they would leave their computer cameras focused on their faces all night so that if one of them should ever wake up it would be to the face of the other. They would eat dinner together in front of their computers so they could have a meal at the same time, even if that meant Mike would have to have his dinner twice because of the time difference. And they fought, in that they would write frenetic messages to each other on Messenger and through email, and some-times they would get on camera to say things to each other as well.

Bianca not only let Ally read through their online conversa-tions, she wanted her to. 'Now, it doesn't matter if you believe in a higher power or not, fate is testing the two of us,' wrote Mike. 'If we can stand the test of time and hold firm even in the centre of doubt, then together you and I will be able to overcome any obsta-cle.' Ally felt like an emotional voyeur, and was sceptical about Mike's words. How easy it was to let loose with lines of flattery, of sentiment; and what temporary joy they bought before habitual feelings of doubt would seep in again. But then Mike was there all the time, during all hours of the morning and evening. Every time Bianca switched on the computer, he would be there, keen as a labrador, wagging his tail at the sight of her face. And now every time Ally came to visit Bianca, his face would be behind the camera staring back at them, interjecting in their conversations with funny quips or remarks. Pretty soon he became a presence in both their lives. He was always around, but the beauty of it was that he was not an obtrusive boyfriend. Always genial, always conversational, but never physically annoying. Easily switched on or off.

'He always gets a bit down when I close the cams after he falls asleep,' Bianca said, 'because he likes waking up to see me sleeping.' But seeing someone on the screen – albeit all the time – was not the same as a real flesh-and-blood human, Bianca told her.

But then Bianca spoke about the days without make-up, and the day when Mike stood before her in his boxers. 'I feel so fat and ugly,' Bianca had told him, and he said to her, 'I've got something to show you.' He turned around slowly so that every angle was visible to the camera. 'This is me.' The rawest insecurities that they had each been incubating were slaughtered with every kind word, every motion of acceptance. The parentheses of her hips were beautiful to him. 'I love bigger women,' he told her, which made Bianca cry. Slowly and steadily, Bianca began walking tall. She held her chin up, went from mollusc to butterfly. She went for a job interview and got the job.

'Been nursing a sick rat,' Bianca wrote to him one Sunday. Bianca kept two pet rats in her tiny room in Coburg for company, because the landlords did not allow tenants to keep dogs. She brought her rats grainy treats from pet stores, and they had a little wheel in their cage. She changed their newspaper every day. She would also pay over a hundred dollars for their medical treatment if they fell sick, and drive alone around the darkened night streets for hours and hours on end when one of them died. Sometimes she would stop at KFC and buy herself something to assuage the grief.

Bianca told Mike that she was taking care of her rat, Ebony, with knowledge she'd gained from an animal nursing course at TAFE. She hadn't finished the course because that year her mother had decided to kick her out of home.

'Is it working?' he asked.

'A little … she's not well though, she can't control her bladder, she's shaking, losing weight, just sluggish. When I get home, for the past three days I've put her in my jacket pocket to give her my body warmth and have the heater on a little bit towards me … She fell asleep in my hoodie pocket tonite. Wanna see something cute?'

'Okay.'

'Okay, look.'

'Awwww.' He could see the tail peeking out from Bianca's pocket.

'I feel like a kangaroo with a pouch.'

The next evening, Ebony was dead. Bianca turned on the computer, and sure enough Mike was there waiting up for her.

'Wanna see how I found her?' she typed.

'Alright, show me.'

She positioned the camera so it faced the rat cage.

'She died in her sleep,' he reassured her.

'Your eyes always get red and puffy when you cry,' he wrote. 'It's like they're allergic to tears.'

He was quite poetic at times without realising it.

'Did Riley get to school yet?' Bianca would ask Mike in the mornings. Riley was Mike's six-year-old son. Bianca once went to Playtime and won him a whole set of cartoon character plush figurines. She also sent flash cards to help Riley with his spelling and learning.

'Yeah, I woke up, got him dressed, got him his meds, and got him on the bus.'

'Riley really shouldn't be on meds,' she wrote back to him.

'He's too young.'

'Riley acted up on the bus again today, so he got kicked out this week. Now he has to go to school by taxi again,' wrote Mike.

One day Bianca told Ally that Mike had amassed a $600 mobile phone bill calling her up. She said that Mike had telephoned her so often only because he loved her and wanted to hear her voice, even when she was at work. She took it as a sign of love, and sent money over through PayPal.

Slowly, however, signs were emerging that didn't sound all that flash. Bianca tallied them up:

He was unemployed.

He still lived with his parents.

He used to rob houses.

He had full-time responsibility for his son, Riley, who had behavioural problems and learning disorders.

But she did not tell Ally.

The lack of sleep began to create irritations for both she and Mike. They were real lovers, in that they could not switch off from each other. No longer was it a matter of turning off a screen – the person behind it had become real. One problem with this new-found realness was that now everyone else online seemed equally real too. 'It hurts me when you flirt with the other men on camera,' Mike confessed, 'like when they ask you if you will get it on with them and you say, yeah okay, come on.'

'It's a joke,' protested Bianca, 'they know that you and I are together. Come on, it says very clearly on my MySpace profile that I am with you.'

They had been together for nine months. But it was time to get real, because contentment rested on the concrete things. She sent him a maths textbook because he was studying for a test. He had enrolled in a course to be an electrician, but he told her how hard it was to learn from a book: 'For me I have to have it explained to me. Then I can just stare at the lips of the person talking and keep focused that way.' He claimed to have attention deficit disorder but with her this disability seemed to drop away.

Bianca had influenced Mike in ways that made him better too. It was like she had given him a boot up the arse to make him realise that he could not rest so easy. That he had to fight for things in life, just as she had. He found a job. He was becoming focused. After twenty-seven years, he was becoming a man. But that also meant that he could not spend all waking hours in front of the camera: 'I need to work this weekend because this union job is going to cost money to start. I just want you to stand behind me on it.'

But she could not get used to him not being around. 'We hardly get to have fun together anymore,' she wrote to him. 'You're now always too tired.' She would cry and he would design Photoshop drawings to say sorry. After a few days, things would be better again. This went on for a few more months, until Bianca decided that where there was a will, there would be a way.

Bianca had never been overseas before, but she decided that sometime in March she would go to America. Or they could meet in the middle, in Hawaii. She looked up hotels where she could stay. She checked out the plane fares. To make it official, they would tell all their online friends. 'Imagine,' said Bianca, 'when we finally meet up, we could set our screens together and everyone online will see us together in the same place.'

Bianca said that now things were in gear, it would work. This rough patch in the quilt of their relationship did not need to snare. It was just one little square out of hundreds of possible permutations of colours and possibilities. 'And just how are we going to make it work?' he wrote back. 'When you visit I'll be working days and going to classes at night.'

The final bad sign, the one Ally knew meant doom for Bianca, was this: when Bianca had already ordered her passport, he decided that he did not want to meet her.

'If you want to break up with me then that's okay,' Bianca hammered into the keyboard, 'but I want to see your face. This isn't a conversation of seeing walls or feet, etc.' The glyphs of their typing started to look like sharp teeth. He shifted the camera higher so she could see his face. And then he said: 'This really isn't going to work.'

He wasn't looking at her face. He was looking straight into a camera.

Afterwards, Bianca felt like she had swallowed boiled eggs too fast.

It was the same feeling she had when she was eight and ate all those Mars bars. For her eighth birthday, Bianca's father had bought her forty-eight of them. He'd got them for her from the NQR store. This was the time before the invention of the Fun Size nuggets, sealed in plastic – though how anything that small could be called fun was beyond Bianca. Bianca's forty-eight birthday Mars bars were the full size. Her father gave them to her in one go, and she ate them all within a week because she was an eight-year-old child. Now Bianca could never touch a Mars bar ever again.

'Bad things come in threes,' she told Ally as they sat on Bianca's bed. 'First my rat dies, and now Mike breaks up with me. I bet I will lose my job next.' Bianca had the computer on her lap and glared into it, checking every possible chat room and message board and site where Mike could be. Looking for the final sign. She did this for about a week. One day, sure enough, it came. It was as if the corners of her universe had contracted, imploded, folded in on themselves.

Mike had turned his MySpace profile to single again.

24/7

My friend Bianca promised to drive me to the 24-hour Kmart in East Burwood, because I wanted to see what people need to buy at three in the morning. Bianca goes for long drives alone, late at night, when she cannot get to sleep. On these drives, she discovers such places.

She was named after Mick Jagger's first wife, because her parents liked the name and they liked the Rolling Stones. We'd grown up around the block from each other, in Braybrook, a suburb filled with factories and steel-framed skeletons of stripped-away buildings. When I was a child my parents kept me carefully reined, between four walls; Bianca was free to wander the streets, carefully, but at will. Her driving habits are similar.

At 11.15 pm, Bianca turns off the Burwood Highway, and suddenly we have arrived. It is a massive building rising out of the dark, and the blue and red sign is like sky-graffiti, with the 'K' kicking through the night. The letters spell out a landmark loiterer's paradise in the middle of dark suburbia.

Burwood is the site where Australia's first Kmart opened, in 1969. The store's slogan is 'Where good times start', and when it debuted, this flagship American import was flooded with ladies in pillbox hats and twin-sets. The car park was jammed with

HD Holdens and Valiants, and people lined up for the promise of good times. But the good times could only stretch for so long before they snapped back, like gum chewed too long, and became tasteless.

Tonight, this place filled with polymer and polyester goods no longer promises excitement for its temporary inhabitants. It has become an alleviator of our boredom. Tonight, the store is so shiny spick-and-span that we forget we are standing inside a piece of Australian history. At 11.30, when we walk through the automatic doors, it is as if it is still daytime. The first inanimate object of consumer desire we see perpetuates this delusion: out the front, in the foyer, is a Professional Titanium barbeque displayed for the special price of $599. I wonder if anyone has ever thought of the Great Australian Outdoor Eating Dream at two in the morning, and decided to buy one.

There are whole families inside the store: wide-eyed kids staring at shelves in the toy section, a small boy on a yellow scooter. Dads examining gardening tools and mums loading their trolleys with discounted tissue boxes. People looking at the most ordinary and useful things in life: small clock radios, car fresheners, tween under-wear, fishing equipment, adhesive rolls of book covering, eggtimers. Here, time is suspended, and such scrutiny takes on an extra dimen-sion. I realise how deeply complex shopping complexes are.

The Dalai Lama once confided that if he were not mindful, he could become dangerously attached to visiting supermarkets: 'Everywhere I look, I see so many beautiful things.' Inside this store, everywhere I look is the work of a million different people from all around the globe. Bianca and I marvel at all the things a person could own, produced en masse by people we will never meet. This is everything we ever wanted when we were young, our giant play-ground, except that now we are cashed-up, sort of. We spend hours trawling through every aisle, trying on clothes we aren't going to buy because they aren't on sale yet. We can get our photos developed at three in the morning, if we so desire. In the confectionery section Bianca gets false teeth and a pair of lips, while I choose a packet of muffin mix.

Now there are no pillbox hats, but pillboxes on discount for 50 cents, and twin-sets come in enormous plastic-wrapped bundles from the factory floors of China. Now, people come to Kmart in their pyjama bottoms, like the Chinese students we see ahead of us: two young men and a young woman with fashionably dyed hair. The boy is dressed in flannelette bottoms and has black-rimmed glasses. The girl is wearing a dressing gown. Sleepy-faced, they swim half-dazed through the bright lights to find their distractions. They walk through the store with the familiarity of someone rummaging through their fridge at night.

Following them down the aisles, I pause and become smitten with cheap nylon yarn that comes in the colours of lollies and the texture of feathers. Lost in a revelry of future scarves, I realise after a while that I have lost my three Chinese students. I glance around and see that Bianca has disappeared, too. Looking at my watch, I realise that it is already 12.26. I wander over to a sales assistant, a pretty teenager whose face is deliberately aged by Maybelline. She is attaching stickers to boxes of DVDs.

'What do people buy at three in the morning?' I ask.

'Oh, you'd be surprised. The big-ticket items they don't usually buy during the day. PlayStations. Bedding and manchester. Sometimes bicycles.'

'What about barbeques?'

'Yes ...' She pauses. 'But not often, because they need to be delivered, and people at night like things they can drive home with in the back of their car.'

I ask her about her shift, and she tells me that she began only half an hour ago, and works until 8 am. She says that she enjoys this shift because it is more relaxed.

A middle-aged Vietnamese couple passes us. They are decent-looking people dressed in Kmart tracksuit pants, mildly marauding the aisles searching for household goods: pillows, chairs, mirrors, tumblers ($3 for twelve long glasses). Two Indian men have sacks of beanbag stuffing in their trolley and are wheeling it to the register. Along the way, there is a shatter: they have accidentally knocked over a tray of tumblers with the trolley. The security guard near the front register approaches them, probably to tell them to pay for the damage.

At around 1 am, there is a fifteen-minute reconciliation. This is the only time that the registers are put on hold and customers cannot make purchases. We are warned far in advance of these fifteen minutes by the in-store PA system, which interrupts the in-store radio broadcast. A soundtrack of music, news updates and promotional segments is the backdrop to this buyers' heaven.

Bianca drove us here partly because she wanted a blender to make smoothies. She gets one with a glass cup for $35. We don't feel like consumers, because we can muck around here until daybreak if we want. We line up at the cashier at 3.14, and I tally up what I have brought: a striped jumper for my sister, a red cardigan for me, a tin of blush for Bianca, a lamington tray, my packet of muffin mix, a scrubbing brush with a holder shaped like a blue frog, a pencil-case for my brother and a toilet block that smells like lavender. I had only meant to accompany Bianca on her trip, and write about the strange things people brought at strange times. But somehow, surreptitiously, in the slow dreaming hours, Kmart has seduced me into becoming her shopping accomplice. Bianca and I emerge into the sharp navy night and head towards the car, feeling strangely excited and fulfilled. We cannot wait to open our white plastic bags.

SPIRIT CHIMES

Back during a time when music did not have many layers but only a few austere notes, a time when the white noise of life was the noise of industry, the ancient Chinese turned their grain scoop upside down. This transformed a practical object into a musical instrument with a double purpose. Bells were hung in the corners of large pagodas to scare away birds and evil spirits. During the Han dynasty, morning bells and dusk drums sounded every day to help the Chinese keep regularity over their lives and work. Old Beijing was made up of narrow alleyways shaped in a grid. Inside each grid was a microcosm of a small community made up of court-yard houses. High walls covered everything so you could not see what your neighbour was up to. Overlooking this ancient city was the Drum and Bell Tower, China's largest and highest timekeeper.

According to legend, an official named Deng was commissioned to cast the bell of the tower, but each new casting came out wrong. The bell would not reverberate. Almost a year had elapsed and the emperor was getting impatient, so one evening Deng's daughter threw herself into the molten bronze as a sacrifice to the gods. Her father could only salvage one of her embroidered slippers before she disappeared into the furnace. The next day, the casting was a success. The emperor named her Goddess of the Golden

Furnace and built a temple in her honour. Now when the bell rings, the holler of its echo sounds like the Chinese word for shoe, *xie*. Mothers tell small children that the goddess is searching for her missing slipper.

I had never thought much about bells until I visited the land of my ancestors. Seeing bells everywhere, I realised how historically integral they were to Chinese culture. During the day the Beijing Bell Tower stood majestically, but at night it was mesmerising in a different manner. Under the faint orange glow of nearby street lamps, the tower rose from the streets, an unimaginably big black block, a frightening dark place of panic. It seemed to fill up half the sky. I crossed the street to avoid looking at it.

During times of war, bell metal – the hard bronze alloy used for making bells – was melted down to make cannons. 'Hear the loud alarm bells – brazen bells! What tale of terror, now, their turbulency tells!' wrote Edgar Allan Poe in his frenetic poem.

In ancient times, bells were also used to warn about wars. In 1384, the bell tower of Xi'an marked the geographical centre of the city, the old capital of China. It was built by Emperor Zhu Yuanzhang as a way to dominate the surrounding countryside and provide early warning of attack by rival rulers. This is one of the reasons why for centuries, Xi'an was known by the name Cheng'an, the Land of Perpetual Peace. During times of peace, cannons were melted down to make bells. The area where the Hiroshima Peace Memorial Park in Japan now stands had once been the busiest downtown district before the atomic bombing. After the bomb, all that was left of the site was a big open field. This empty grey vacuum became the location for the Memorial Park.

The domed belfry of the Park's Peace Bell represents the universe, and its surface is engraved with a map of the world with no boundaries. When the Greek Embassy donated the bell in

1964, they chose a quote from Socrates to be inscribed on it. The quote was only two words: 'Know thyself.'

According to the inscription on the Hiroshima Peace Bell, it is difficult enough to know oneself and one's own motivations, let alone control the actions of others. I found this out the hard way when I went on retreat to the Dharma Drum Mountain Buddhist Chan (Zen) Meditation Centre in Templestowe. At 4.30 am, the morning bell would ring. Wordlessly, we would get out of bed, go outside when the sky was still dark, and do yoga exercises to prepare our sleepy muscles for sitting. And then we would head inside the Meditation Hall, and sit with our faces towards the wall.

The bell would ring again to signal the beginning of meditation. Crossed-legged in full-lotus position so our feet were locked, we could not move. We faced the blank wall, prepared to slowly and painfully learn patience. It was there that I realised how we could simultaneously love and loathe the only sound during our retreat, the sound of the bell. It was loathed when it depleted us of sleep, of agency, and when it interfered with our ego. When the sound of singing metal told us that our hour was up, reassured us that we could untangle our legs and ease out of physical pain and mental discomfort, it was loved. How could we feel so strongly ambivalent about an object with no independent personality or even life? Were we going mad? The Bangalore poet Tagore wrote that 'we read the world wrong, and say that it deceives us'. We weren't going mad, we were just realising how most suffering and joy is often self-created, and testing the limits of our tolerance for the world beyond our control.

When the world spiralled beyond her control, Sylvia Plath wrote her semi-autobiographical book about feeling like she was trapped beneath an instrument designed so that no sound could emerge from the airless environment. *The Bell Jar* is an apt metaphor for the way patients with mental illness were handled during the early days of mental health treatment in America. Asylums commonly shackled people suffering from mental illness with iron cuffs around their ankles, and chains attached to their wrists. Eventually, with better understanding, this practice stopped – although lobotomies and electric-shock treatments were still performed regularly during Plath's short lifetime. In 1953, the National Mental Health Association made a call out to all the asylums to donate their discarded chains and shackles. These were melted down and recast into the Mental Health Bell, a signal of hope, made from the same bindings that once imprisoned patients.

Poe, who seemed to have suffered a number of undiagnosed mental illnesses in his lifetime, referenced bells continually in his work, as if the instrument of clashing alloy was driving him to distraction. After reading *The Bells*, I also started to notice the modern incarnations of the bell in my day-to-day life in Melbourne: the electronic ringing of the alarm clock in the morning when I was trying to sleep. The cry of bicycle bells to cars backing out of driveways. The dinging of railway crossings. The annoying ringtones of mobile phones on the tram while I was trying to read a book. And of course, the common sounds of school bells, church bells and prayer bells, all summoning people to assembly or action in the most inconspicuous manner possible. The bell, I realised, was the most overlooked object of popular control in modern society.

But this is not surprising when we look back at the history and culture of what bells have done, or made people do, for better or for worse. Although Shakespeare's Macbeth contemplates regicide, it is finally a bell that compels him to commit the deed: 'the bell invites me. Hear it not, Duncan; for it is a knell / That summons thee to heaven or to hell.'

In 1612 a tailor named Robert Dow left an odd annual endowment to the Church of St Sepulchre in London – a fitting name for its long relationship with the nearby Newgate Prison. After his death, Dow wanted to ensure that the condemned knew their punishment and got a proper admonition before they headed to the gallows. So he specified that the bellman of the church should ring the bell on the eve of every execution day, and to ring it again as the cart carrying the condemned left Newgate for the Tyburn gallows the following morning. On the midnight before the executions, the sextant walked solemnly through the passageway between the church and the prison, and stood outside the cells of the condemned. There, he rang the bell twelve times and recited a warning prayer. I wonder whether this was what Poe meant when he writes of 'the people – ah, the people – They that dwell up in the steeple / all alone / and who tolling, tolling, tolling / In that muffled monotone, / Feel a glory in so rolling / On the human heart a stone.'

Bells are now rung in churches, monasteries, abbeys, temples and synagogues on the day of execution for American death-row prisoners, but for a different reason. The seventeenth-century English poet John Donne perhaps had a clear and enlightened idea of how interconnected human beings were when he penned the lines: 'any man's death diminishes me, because I am involved in Mankinde; And therefore never send to know for whom the bell tolls; It tolls for thee.'

Nine years ago, a Dominican nun named Dorothy Briggs started the 'For Whom the Bell Tolls' campaign as 'a reminder to all who hear them that all of us are diminished by continuing acts of state-sponsored murder'. The campaign will continue until the death penalty is abolished in America.

For America – unlike Europe, with its dark medieval history of bells foreshadowing doom – the bell is a symbol of hope and progress. Its most famous is the Liberty Bell, cast in 1752 with a quote from the Bible inscribed on it: 'Proclaim LIBERTY throughout all the Land unto all the Inhabitants thereof. Lev. XXV X.'

The Liberty Bell gained iconic importance when the abolitionists adopted it as their symbol, since the following lines of Leviticus 25:10 include the directive: 'and ye shall return every man unto his possession, and ye shall return every man unto his family'.

When I returned to Australia, I learnt that we too had our own world-famous bell. Once the holding camp for Japanese and Italian prisoners of war during World War II, the NSW town of Cowra is now home to the bronze World Peace Bell, one of only seven in the world. The 103 member states of the United Nations gifted coins from their own countries, which were then melted down and cast into the bell. It is rung to commemorate World Peace Day on the third Tuesday of every September.

There is something eternal about an instrument that only plays a single note. But never underestimate the power of that one note. When the largest swinging bell ever cast by the United States in the nineteenth century chimed in the steeple of Saint Francis De Sales Church in Cincinnati for the first time, it took six men to swing the clapper. The resultant E-flat shattered nearby windows. The clapper was never used again: today, the bell is rung only with a small hammer tapping its rim.

Yoke, crown, head, shoulder, waist, lip, mouth, bead line. And finally, the clapper. Who knew that the terminology used to describe such an ordinary and ancient – but not archaic – object could be so poetic and sensuous? Who knew a bell could holler so loudly? Cry so plaintively? Induce a person to paroxysms of tears, or press a fingertip upon the bruise of their basest fears? Bells are rung at weddings and sounded at funerals. In that singular note, they speak of the passage of time, of beginnings and endings, the order of society, a people's struggle for freedom and independence, a faith's emblem of human enlightenment, a person's quest for sanity, hope and liberty. And ultimately, they also stop people from being run over by trains when they are too busy listening to their mobile ringtones.

Yoke, crown, head, shoulder, waist, lip, mouth, bead lines of sweat. This could also describe the parts of the maiden as she disappeared into the flames, so important was that casting of the bell to the ancient Chinese.

HAIR APPARENT

Mr Abe Lourie is eighty-one, and tells me that he is in perfect health. Every morning he walks up two flights of stairs to open his store. The lift has been broken for quite some time and yet customers continue to come up, because for half a century he has helped fill a lack in people's lives. Stacked from floor to ceiling with over a thousand heads of real and synthetic hair, Creative Wigs is one of those places that reminds you of a time before the merged business – a time of the butcher, the baker and the wigmaker.

Though Mr Lourie does not make the wigs he sells, he talks about hairpieces with a reverence otherwise reserved for miraculous modern drugs, paracetamol and gentle herbal balms to alleviate persistent aches. Mr Lourie used to be a pharmacist fifty years ago, on the corner of Swanston and Bourke streets. 'Around that time, exciting people were beginning to arrive in Melbourne,' he says. 'Entertainers used to come down from the Southern Cross Hotel.' His business changed forever when a Hong Kong supplier came into his pharmacy with two human-hair samples. One was a ponytail and the other was a black hair-switch. Mr Lourie put them in the window and by the end of the week they were gone.

'Look at this,' he exclaims, as he shows me a bobbed synthetic wig with a handmade monofilament front. 'This is the difference between an ordinary wig and a good one.' I see that the hair is handwoven, four strands at a time, through the transparent lace mesh at the front of the wig. When I put my hand beneath the wig, the mesh between the hair is invisible, showing only skin. Exactly like scalp. A person wearing one of these wigs could part their hair on any side of their head.

Mr Lourie's daughter, Diane, is attending to a woman sitting in front of the mirror in the middle of the showroom, offering her wigs of different lengths. Nestled between the wings of her new hair, the lady's expression is one of quiet astonishment – she cannot believe this is fake hair. 'My real hair never looked so good,' the lady jokes to me. Diane helps her part it in the direction she prefers; it feels more like being at the hairdresser than in a warehouse.

'Although we are generally a wholesaler, every day we will have about four or five people come in who are undergoing chemotherapy treatment,' Diane tells me later. 'People who've never worn wigs before tend to ask for human hair, but a human-hair wig needs to be taken to a hairdresser to be cut and permed. So I advise them to get synthetic wigs, which already come styled and are much easier to manage.'

Each wig has a different name, labelled on the hundreds of cardboard boxes stacked neatly around the store – Felicity, Shilo, Tatum, Miranda, Angelica, Ryan, Leah – like little folded personalities in hibernation. Sylvia, Mr Lourie's longest-serving employee, has been working at the store for more than three decades. She shows me a box of tiny wigs for children with cancer and alopecia. 'Usually the kids come in with their mums and dads. Girls come in more often than boys, because losing their hair affects them more.'

There are also ringmaster moustaches and Salvador Dalí moustaches, mutton chops for the sides of the face, toupees to be pinned onto thinning hair and even chest hair made of human hair hand-sewn into a lace mesh, to be adhered with liquid adhesive.

'Who would buy chest hair?' I ask.

'People in the movie business,' Mr Lourie replies.

Over the years, hair from his store has graced the heads and bodies of the casts of *Lord of the Rings, Braveheart, Moulin Rouge!* and *The Matrix,* as well as the Australian productions of musicals such as *Priscilla: Queen of the Desert, Chicago* and *The Phantom of the Opera.*

'I never thought this job would get so interesting,' Sylvia says. 'Back in the '80s, Jon Bon Jovi came with his crew and all their girlfriends. They wanted to visit Brighton Beach and so needed disguises. We gave them big moustaches and caps with hair hanging down the back.' Pictures of celebrities adorn the place but they are stuck on the walls more like thank-you cards than advertisements. Many are signed, and Mr Lourie points one out to me. 'Vivien St James,' he says with sincere affection, 'was a great lady.' Mr Lourie then tells me about meeting her when she was a shy young man who came into a wig shop for the first time. The original Les Girls and Danny La Rue, BABBA and Björn Again have also been regular visitors.

Yet this is not a place of hyperbole. There is none of the 'you-look-fabulous-darling!' flamboyancy of the glass-windowed salons and wig stores of the suburbs. Mr Lourie has a chemist's care in labelling and shelving his stock, and the gaze of a doctor with an untarnished history of accurate diagnoses. When not tending to customers, the Louries keep busy doing other things, such as filling wig orders for hospitals.

'Sometimes,' Diane tells me, 'we will get Jewish ladies coming in for *sheitels,* though not that often. Some of them will have no problem sitting in front of Dad to be fitted for a wig.' And who wouldn't feel at ease here, in this quiet upper-storey warehouse in front of a man who takes as much attentive care with his transformative stock of human relief as the pharmacist he was trained to be?

The cabinet next to Mr Lourie's desk is stacked with photographs of his grandchildren, one of whom works with him in the store. 'I have no intention of retiring,' he finally tells me, 'because there is no one in Australia who knows more about wigs than I do.'

When I leave, Sylvia is adjusting a wig to fit the size of the wearer's head – cutting out tufts of hair and sewing it with a needle and thread.

ALLY OF THE DOLLS

She was found beneath the floorboards of an old house in Geelong, and appeared to have been through a fire. Her body had disintegrated, but her head was still intact. She was from England, and probably came into existence sometime between 1908 and 1925 – though Barb, who discovered her, cannot be sure. She still has a faint bloom on her face, even though she is not alive.

'That's her original blush,' Barb tells me, 'painted on before the porcelain was glazed and fired in the kiln. These Diamond Pottery bisque-head dolls can also survive a century of being immersed in water, and their faces would still look the same.' Barb points to the eyes: 'Those are also original – they were found sunken in the back of her skull, because of the heat from the fire.' I look at the aquarium starbursts in the doll's irises. Her upper and lower eyelashes make them look like splay-legged insects.

Barb and her husband, Bob, run the Little Doll House Museum in Port Fairy, on Victoria's Great Ocean Road. All the figures on display are from Barb's own collection; her twenty-two years of rescuing and adopting have resulted in an orphanage for more than 1300 dolls, whose lives span three centuries.

There is a Zen koan that asks the impossible question: what was your original face before your parents were born? There is something special about making an object in the image of ourselves. A dear friend of mine, who was born in London during the Blitz, told me the story of her first 'doll': a small postcard of Rodin's *The Kiss* that she found when she was four. She was so awed by the beauty of something she could not yet explain that she made a matchbox bed for her naked marbled friends, and begged her mum for a scrap of material to keep them warm.

When I enter the museum, there are only a few other visitors, even though the $2 entry fee is waived for children on weekends: an old woman named Yvonne, who has brought in her doll for valuation, and a mother with her two small daughters.

'Do you want to see something really, really old?' Barb asks the girls.

'This doll used to be my grandmother's,' Yvonne explains, letting the six-year-old pat her family heirloom's flaxen head. Doll shops arouse feelings of familial feminine kinship – after all, dolls are mostly made in the image of women, children and babies. Ken is never as popular as Barbie.

Barb carefully inspects the beautiful doll, peering into its eternally bewildered eyes. She values it at $450. 'Wow,' gasps one of the girls.

'I'm not going to sell it, dear,' Yvonne says. 'I'm going to pass it down to my granddaughter.'

'Make sure you take a photograph of your doll, and write on the back of it how you got her, whom she was from and when she got a change of clothes,' Barb advises. 'A doll carries with it the family history.'

Barb was once a window dresser in Melbourne, and the dolls are arranged like panels of artwork, behind glass cabinets. Some are like impressionist paintings rendered in three dimensions, with Renoir faces, while others are simply Gauguin: primitive, raw and weird.

There is a French boudoir doll with long blue eyes and an exotic heart-shaped face that reminds me of William Morris's women.

The specimens in the Australian-doll cabinet are practical princesses that double as tea cosies and toilet-roll covers. There are also kewpie dolls – prizes from long-ago shows – and Aussie icons: Plucka Duck, Kylie Mole, Con the Fruiterer, Ozzie Ostrich. There is the Irwin family, with Bindi in wholesome khaki, snuggled up against a koala.

And then there are the celebrity dolls: Michael Jackson and Macaulay Culkin in the same cabinet, Macaulay with hands adhered to face in *Home Alone* pose, a disturbingly precocious caricature of Munch's *The Scream*. An elegant Jackie Kennedy stands tall among skanky *Little Britain* dolls that expectorate obscenities when you pull a string on their backs. 'Thank God they are behind glass,' the girls' mother comments.

The oldest doll, from 1850, has a wax face covering a papier-mâché skull. Her arms are made entirely of leather; it looks as if she's wearing kidskin gloves. 'Someone's grandmother gave it to them in their will. The old lady had looked after it all her life, and the granddaughter did not want it – she had it sitting in the trunk of her car. It could have melted!' Barb tells us in horror. She has been to countless expos and antique shops and country fairs to rescue dolls. And there are some strange ones, not least the so-called Mongoloid doll, whose red-amber eyes, mean arched brows and pursed persimmon lips are terrifying. All the other celluloid dolls in the cabinet, with their innocuous water-blue or beetle-brown eyes, seem to look away or stare ahead.

Barb tells me about these dolls, made between the 1880s and 1950s. She cradles one from the 1920s that is wearing a hand-crocheted outfit. His nose was bitten by a child, and his fingers, too. He is highly flammable, which is why they stopped producing his infant brethren, and Barb handles him like a real baby. 'These were called feather dolls. Feel how light he is.' As she passes him to me, she mentions that she never had such a doll when she was young, which is why she takes good care of them now.

Nearby, there is a Princess Diana doll wearing an exact replica of the famous wedding dress, which won its creator first prize at the Melbourne Doll Show.

'When we were growing up, it was our dream to have a bride doll,' the mother tells her two girls.

'I suppose that's not every girl's dream now,' Barb remarks.

'No, they prefer these,' I joke, pointing to some scantily clad Bratz dolls.

'They have mean faces,' the older girl says. 'I don't like them.'

'They look like the types of girls you wouldn't want to be friends with at school,' their mum says.

At the Barbie-doll cabinet, we see Barbie as Scarlett O'Hara; as a fairy from *The Lord of the Rings*, flirting with Legolas; and as Lucille Ball, winking at an Elvis on the same shelf. 'Now, a real Barbie collector would never take these dolls out of their boxes,' Barb says, 'because once a doll is out of its packaging, it immediately loses its value. It's like driving an expensive sports car out of the dealer's garage, I suppose.' Barbie's body was pilfered from Lilli, a small swimsuited doll from Germany, originally made to amuse men. A co-founder of Mattel brought Lilli to America, renamed her and mass-marketed the doll to little girls. It is said that around the world, three Barbies are sold every second.

Before I leave, I buy a little child doll for $3. On the tag is a note: 'Some hair problems.' In the 1970s, an owner took to her with a pair of scissors. I think she looks better with the straw-blond mop hacked back, anyway. I fall in love with her the moment I set eyes on her red dress and spotted pinafore. She is kneeling, as if in prayer, curved feet resting against her bottom. Her lips are fluted for a reverent kiss, and her hands are raised. Save for her pose, she looks like the girl in Rodin's *Eternal Idol* made plastic, without her lover.

LOOKING SHEEPISH

'Sheep's placenta for the face is all the rage among Chinese women,' my father said. All his mainland-Chinese friends told him that this was the perfect gift for me to give when I went to Beijing: lanolin oil containing adventurous admixtures of animal innards. So Dad scoured the Chinese newspapers, looking at the ads of shops that cater to overseas travellers. We drove to a place with signs outside in both Chinese and English, and a giant gilt sheep painted on the window.

This was definitely not a tacky knick-knack shop where you could buy ten koalas for two dollars. It was white-lit, like a swanky hotel's bathroom, and the shelves were stacked with bottles and vials and small boxes with gold-font and glossy veneers. These were gifts you give the people overseas with whom you want to be friends. Friends help you when you're in trouble, and the gifts ensure that you remain their friend and not a bothersome foreigner.

'*Ni hao*,' said the mainland-Chinese owner when we entered. 'What are you looking for?' Dad told her, and showed her a newspaper clipping. She led us down the centre aisle, where the lanolin skincare products were sold in pallets of six and eight. The natural oily coating of sheep's wool, lanolin is widely used as a base in cosmetics: it is one of the key ingredients in Oil of Olay, which was invented by a South African chemist (indeed, the product's name is a play on 'lanolin'). Lanolin oil might be 'a gift from nature', as the packaging suggested, but the thought of rubbing the afterbirth of an animal on your face was still disturbing.

The tiny tubs were packaged resplendently, with the green Australian Made logo emblazoned on every box and its kangaroo bouncing with promise of foreign pulchritude. The storeowner had beautiful pallid skin, and I wondered whether she used her own products. '*Hen bai, hen hao,*' she said to me: very white, very good. This is why, when you go into those little sticker-photo booths in Australia's Chinatowns, the flash illuminates like a shock of lightning and everything is washed out except for your eyes, two small nostril spots and a shadowy sliver of mouth. And flat, white, luminous skin.

The skin creams ranged from one to eight dollars a tub. 'Why are they so cheap?' I asked Dad. 'Are you sure the Chinese will use this stuff?'

'Of course,' he said. 'It's made in Australia.'

'Which one is the best?' he asked the owner, as we stared at the dozen or so brands on display. After some thought, we decided on two pallets of the small tubs regally branded Royal Life Placenta Cream, which promised to be a '24-Hour Slow Release Moisturiser'. The packaging had an emblem that looked like a royal crest: a king and queen dressed in togas stood on either side of a shield with a kangaroo and a lamb on it. The queen carried the Australian flag and stood on a strand of wattle. What an odd and yet somehow accurate representation of how the Chinese view this country!

'What about male friends who may help me?' I asked Dad. 'What should we get them? Wallets? Alcohol?'

The owner led us to another shelf, this one containing ointments and medicinal items for boosting every physiological function.

There were the usual substances, like shark-liver oil, snake oil and cod-liver tablets. And there were others of a more arcane variety. Deer Pizzle (second listed ingredient: grape seed) boasted that it contained various minerals to aid circulation and the kidneys. It also gave 'strength and vigour to their manhood'. Who knew that a concoction of Bambi's dangly bits and fruit could have such properties? Then I remembered that I was going to a country renowned for creating more eunuchs than any other place on Earth – no wonder there was an obsession with pizzles and performance.

I walked past another box, containing the green-lipped mussel, which sounded like a poor creature that had never been kissed when plucked from the bowels of the sea. And there was Deer Velvet, made from deer antlers, also used to boost performance. 'Um, let's not get any of these things,' I said, and Dad concurred.

We walked over to the next section, where lambswool blankets, still with the leather of the skin attached, were draped like white snow. I wondered about the harvesting of sheep's placenta and the fate of these lambs, and whether there was any correlation. 'Not these, either.'

I stood in front of a stack of chocolate boxes. Paton's Macadamia Nuts: surely these would be popular? 'But no one in China has ever heard of this brand,' said Dad, 'so how will they know we haven't picked the cheapest supermarket supplies?' I told him that macadamia nuts were almost exclusively Australian. 'But no one has heard of this nut in China,' Dad told me.

In the end, we decided I would buy the rest of my presents in China. But I also decided to get twenty medium-sized koala bears, each bearing a boomerang, for any children I met overseas.

Driving home, I commented that some of the medicinal products the Chinese like are bizarre, almost voodoo-like. But then I remembered that I have eaten bird's nest, made from the saliva of little birds. I have eaten the webbed feet of duck, and their bills. I have eaten pig's tongue, relishing the feel of the tiny bumpy bits on my tongue, until someone told me what it was and I felt like I had just kissed swine. Mum used to cook pig's intestine – small and large – for us, and the lining of cow's stomach. We used to buy duck-embryo eggs that were sold in the marketplace in Footscray before they were banned. We called them Abortion Eggs, because at the bottom was a little duck foetus curled unto itself, complete with feathered, folded wings. This was all in Australia. I hadn't even reached China yet.

In China I realised that chocolate is scarce and painfully expensive. No wonder the people are so thin. Chips are also a luxury item, and biscuits, and things in packages. The cheapest food is the hawker food: corn, sweet potato, pieces of meat on skewers with the fat barbequed off, skewered lettuce and tofu soaking in chilli. Eating Chinese chocolate is like eating sweetened brown crayons. Next time, I told myself, I would load up with chocolate as gifts.

There were Chinese brands of snake oil and lamb's placenta, but the Western skincare brands were more expensive: Olay, Lancôme, Nivea. These are the brands that very wealthy Chinese women use – except that each product includes 'skin whitening' elements.

My Chinese friends loved the Royal Life cream. They knew exactly what the coveted sheep's placenta was. They opened the packages, unscrewed the lids of the tubs and sniffed the sweetly perfumed white ointment. 'Is this what you use to keep your skin so white?'

'No.' I could not lie. 'I stay inside, working in an office all day, and I also have anaemia.' Although my Mandarin was so rudimentary that I did not have much of a personality in China, I was elated to discover that I had said something funny. I also realised that it was equally strange for the Chinese to see me with my pills laden with preservatives and additives not found in the natural world.

My students loved the koala bears with their boomerangs. On their label, written in large letters, was 'Happy Memories from Australia', but at the very bottom, in tiny print, was the evidence of their Oriental origin. I had unwittingly returned these little creatures to their birthplace.

HOME TRUTHS

THE SHED

The shed was always locked.

Right from when I was about four, I was told never to tell anyone about the metal shed. It whirred and hummed like a live thing. It vibrated like a massive machine with a throbbing migraine heartbeat. 'If you tell anyone, we could get into big trouble from the government,' Mum and Dad always warned. 'The government does not know we do this.'

'What's the government?' I asked.

'People who are good to us,' my father explained, 'but who also take our money.'

'Isn't that stealing?' I imagined cloaked pilferers stalking our house at night, with crowbars ready to break into the shed.

But there was no money in the shed, just a lot of twenty-four-carat gold. So I thought that the government wanted our gold, the gold my mother melted and moulded into shape in that shed. Red dust floated out when the breeze blew, from the gaps beneath the door. In the Australian summer, the shed heated up like a hot poker, and because it did not have any windows that could open, it was difficult for Mum to breathe while she was in there.

Mum spent most of her daylight hours in that shed, and I was never allowed to tell, let alone show anyone, what was inside: the wax moulds, the plaster casts, the grey filings and tiny hills of gold dust on metal trays – remnants from the filing down of rings. When I was four, I used to poke my finger in those gold hills and spread them flat into strange rivers on the tray. 'Aiyoh!' Mum would yell when she saw me. I was not allowed to move or take my hands from the tray lest we lost a bit of the gold dust to the ground. Dad would fill a used ice-cream container with water and soak my fingers in it, so that the gold would un-adhere itself and slowly float to the bottom of the container, where it could be rescued, melted down and reused.

Mum made jewellery in that shed in our backyard. Bespoke jewellery, some of the shops in the inner city would call it. Completely made by hand. Artisan labour, they proclaimed on small tags in the sterling surfaces of the shop counters, and because each item had that little label it could be sold at a hundred times the price of my mother's labour. To make a bracelet, my mother would stretch gold wire until it was almost hair thin. One end of the wire would slip and flick her in the face, and there would be a line of blood. She would then take the wire and sit down at her work desk, which was a white corkboard affair one of our family friends had knocked up for us. Her tools were second- or third-hand, but she used new blades in the surgeon's scalpel to cut the strand of gold wire into tiny pieces of no more than half a centimeter long. Then she would link the tiny segments together with a pair of tweezers, as children string Christmas paper chains together with scissors and tape. She would treat it in potassium cyanide and polish the surfaces with a piece of jade that was stuck on a wooden handle.

'One dollar a ring,' Mum would promise us when we were young, 'if you help me polish them.' But she never gave us the money – she just counted up all the rings we had polished. 'Five dollars,' she would tell us, tallying up our halfhearted palely polished efforts, efforts she would always have to fix. 'Five dollars will get you an umbrella.' Then she would come home with one that had Spoony on it, which was the Chinese counterfeit of Charles Schulz's creation. But I didn't want Mum's practical protection from the elements. My seven-year-old self took umbrage at that umbrella. I wanted the five dollars in hand, damn it, I wanted to be paid like a proper Asian back-shed worker so I could use my ill-gotten gain to get a Babie doll, the poor man's version of Barbie. Babie looked like Barbie, but all her hair lifted up at the back so she had a severe undercut, as if she were auditioning to join a white supremacist gang, and when she sat down her legs splayed wide like the fingers of my hand, showing Mum how much I was due to be paid, in a pathetic attempt to procure cash from her instead of an umbrella.

Mum used that umbrella when it rained and she had to deliver her wares. Mum did not deliver her wares to the shops in the inner city because the upmarket clientele of Collins Street was a completely foreign world. The Paris end of Melbourne, they called it, where women walked around with faces like Chanel ads. The kind of beauty that would leak down their necks if it rained. I don't even think Mum had been up there more than once in her life. She was more used to the markets of Phnom Penh and Saigon. Carrying the Spoony umbrella and fake Gucci handbag (that my brother had brought her from China) into a Collins Street jewellery store would mean that the carefully coiffeured ladies would be speaking about her long after she had left. Although Mum's jewellery was entirely handmade, she transported it around wrapped in McDonald's napkins in her fifteen-dollar handbag, and she never wore make-up.

She delivered the hard, shining fruits of her labour to places along the small shopping strips of suburbs brimming with South-East Asians:

the Vietnamese, the Cambodians, the ethnic Chinese. She would set her bag on their narrow glass counters, below which was displayed bright red velvet dotted with coveted twenty-four-carat gold: pendants shaped like Mercedes-Benz signs, rings with dragons and Buddhas on them, blingy necklaces with chains as thick as my little finger.

My brother and I would sit on the chairs reserved for customers who needed their pieces adjusted on the spot – rings too large or bracelets too short. 'When will you be done?' we would whine. 'When will you be done, Mum?' We would walk towards the trays of gold behind the cabinets and breathe on the glass.

Mum was trying to do business, so this time she handed me four dollars and told me to go two stores down to buy pork bread rolls from the Vietnamese bakery. We came back with the food and sat back down. We peeled back the white paper bags and bit into the bread. 'Aiyoh!' Mum yelled at us, 'don't eat in other people's stores!' The store was tiny so all ears were alert. 'Embarrassments to society, that's what you are!' We put the bread away, shut our mouths and learnt to wait. We waited while the jewellery store owners pored over each ring.

'This one's a good one,' Mum told the owner earnestly. 'Kim Heng from the other store ordered seventeen of those.' I looked at the little pendants with the massive faces of Jesus rendered in three-dimensional twenty-four-carat gold and wondered why I never saw anyone wear such a thing. Some of the rings even had tiny emerald or blue cubic zirconias in the eye sockets.

The store owner, a Vietnamese man, turned the pieces around in his hands. His fingers were gnarled like ginseng from his own outworking in the stuffy room near the back of the cramped shop. 'How much?' he asked Mum.

'Four-fifty,' she said. Four-fifty for her four and a half hours of labour.

'Four-fifty, sister?' he repeated.

My mother answered in the affirmative. 'You know that was the price last time I was here.'

'Four-fifty is too much,' said the man.

'What do you mean, too much, brother?'

'Four-fifty is not what the new brother from Cambodia is charging.'

'What new brother from Cambodia?'

'The one who used to be a goldsmith in Cambodia. He brought along some of his old tools. He's been doing it for only six years, but wah! Is he good in his detail! Must be because he's so young.'

Mum shifted her glasses. Mum never used to wear glasses, until her eyesight became shot from too much close work attaching tiny clasps and polishing pendants of the Lord's face with care. Mum didn't know what to say. 'Come on, I've been delivering to you for so long, brother,' Mum cajoled.

It did not work, because the new man had better tools and more nimble fingers.

'The new brother only charges four dollars.'

'But that's ridiculous!'

The small store owner did not say a thing, because there was no need to. He knew that new migrants were desperate to find work and they would settle with any work they could find at any cost. They were just so grateful. And Mum, having worked for over a decade, was not so replete with gratitude or the youthful fervour of ambition. She just wanted the money so we would not be snot-nosed sooks loitering in the streets like she did when she was twelve and they closed down her Chinese school in Cambodia. She wanted to make sure we stayed in school, that we did not need to enter a factory as she did at thirteen.

'Okay. Four dollars then, brother.'

By then, my brother and I had lost interest in the Jesus pendants and even the rings encrusted with red jewels as massive as minor melanomas. We wanted to bite back into our bread rolls. We wanted to leave the sticky seats and the red and gold decor of the store.

But we watched as the store owner measured out ounces of gold on scales, in payment, because he did not have cash on hand that day. Mum had come too early and they had made no sales. Mum watched to make sure that the scales were balanced exactly right, that they were not dodgily weighted in any way. Mum wrote down a few figures of what was owing to her in a small notebook she carried in her handbag. Then she wrapped up the remainder of her wares in the now slightly torn McDonald's napkin, and then the small facecloth.

'Come on, you two, let's go.'

And she led us out down the street to the next store, where the whole scene would repeat itself all over again. But we had learnt to wait.

When I was eight, I hated being eight. I smelled like piss all the time – before my sister was born, my mum's fluorescent yellow pooled on our tiles, because she could not control her bladder when she had babies pushing against her pelvic floor, and after my sister was born her pale yellow streams soaked through the sheets. They did not call us South-East Asians 'yellow' for nothing, I supposed. I lit incense in front of our Buddha shrine – not due to any particular child's faith or piety, but just to disguise the smell of pee from the carpet.

I hated being stuck between the four walls of the house. If I had been born in Cambodia, all my friends my age would have had their babies slung over their backs and we would have played together in the streets. But growing up in sordid suburbia, in a house behind the Invicta carpet factories, my friends came over carrying their Cabbage Patch dolls while I had my sister Alison in my arms. 'Let's go outside and walk to the school and hang around on the monkey bars!' they would tell me, dumping down their dolls on the tiles.

I couldn't do that with Alison. Live babies hollered, and stuff came out of their nappies and stuff came out of their mouths. A baby was cute for half an hour. But to an eight-year-old, that was the limit – after one hour it got a bit tedious, and after a whole day they went home muttering how weird that I had this baby that I could not give back to my mum to look after. Slowly, after a few weeks, my mates petered out, and I knew the only times I would be seeing them was at school. Sometimes their parents would see me balancing a baby on my hip, and once Bianca's dad exclaimed, 'What? Another one?' as if at twelve I was responsible for new progeny in the family.

Mum, like me, was just supposed to be at home watching babies: that was her childhood dream. She narrowly escaped Cambodia's closing acts of the 1970s, when curtains of bombs rained down between the borders to keep out the North Vietnamese, the Vietcong – the Charlies, the Americans called them and wanted to blast them all out of existence. They were so worried the Charlies were hiding in the jungles of the Vietnam–Cambodia border that they didn't care how many Cambodian villagers they would kill in their pursuit of democracy.

My father survived the Cambodian killing fields, emerging as a skin-and-bones man so thin that if he turned sideways he would almost disappear from view. He and my grandmother led the living remnants of his family – his little sister and his wife – through three different countries on foot, sleeping on the floors of jungles when darkness rose. My father calls that trek their three-month backpacker honeymoon, and when they reached the Thai refugee camp, they spent a long sleepy year waiting.

When Mum arrived here, eight months pregnant with me at twenty-two, not knowing a word of English, she began with making jewellery moulds, a sedentary and silent task suitable for new daughters-in-law who've been blessedly deposited in democracies. She made rings by first planting little waxen trees – sometimes sherbet pink, sometimes opal green, growing from waxen stalks that she grew on rubber bases. These waxen trees would be the basis of plaster moulds, which would then be filled with melted gold. After the birth of my brother, she moved on to working with gold. While others saw what dirty work it was and how little ill-gotten gains were to be had, Mum persisted with planting these artificial trees and sawing off their real-gold branches.

When I was fourteen, I realised why we weren't allowed to tell a soul what Mum did, and why Dad had told me once that it was a little like stealing. 'We don't pay taxes on this,' my mother said. 'The government will get us.' The government would tax Mum on her two dollars fifty an hour? That did not make sense even to me. But to illiterate migrants like Mum who were paid cash in hand and asked no questions, it made perfect sense.

Even when the surgeon's scalpel stabbed Mum through the palm so deep that the handle had to be unscrewed to get the blade out, we were not to tell. I remember Mum coming into the house, one hand holding the other like a dead bird. 'The knife stabbed through,' she gasped to Dad. The rims of her eyes were not even red-wet with reflexive tears.

Mum was brave, but it was only later in life that I came to this realisation. When I was young, I didn't care. She was never in the house and I had howling babies to watch over, when all I wanted to do was muck around with my nine-year-old mates.

Two decades later, Mum finally stopped working. I had made it to university, and my three siblings were looking as if they would follow suit.

When Mum stopped working, she discovered she could not be still. Her hands ached to the bone. She had a hacking cough from the potassium cyanide. She had puckered skin on her forearms from third-degree burns of the welding torch and scars from the surgeon's scalpel. Her eyesight was shot, and she needed glasses, which she kept losing, because she never used them to read. She did not read, she could not read.

Mum was locked from the language of the outside world. She had spent two decades in that shed, making those rings and pendants and bracelets. A bracelet would earn her twenty dollars, but it would take her a whole day. That worked out to be a couple of dollars an hour for an eight-hour day. Two dollars fifty does not even get someone a cup of coffee at Starbucks these days. So of course, all our coffee came in massive tins of International Roast from the local Coles supermarket. She would also have tins of sweetened condensed milk in the cupboard, and she mixed it with the coffee and boiling water and gulped cupfuls of that stuff down like there was no tomorrow, even though she knew there was and that it would be exactly the same as the previous day, and the one before that, and the one before that. She woke up each morning blinking at the ceiling of our new house wondering what she would do for the next three decades. Mum was forty, and her life was finally confined to supermarket shopping. That was all. The rest of her world had receded into unintelligible sounds and symbols.

'Your mother's been here twenty years, why doesn't she speak English?' people at the university asked me in bewilderment. There was a group that called themselves the Socialist Alternative and they once invited me to one of their meetings, when one of them in my Global Politics class discovered what my mother did. 'Tell us about how bad it was for your mother,' they urged.

I thought about my mum working for two decades, an active independent business contractor. Then I thought about her not working, lying in bed at home with limp creaking limbs and Zoloft in her bloodstream. 'It wasn't that bad, really.'

We were all seated in a large circle on the floor and there was a cardboard box of organic cooperative food in the middle. One of the Alternative Socialists picked up a roll. 'What do you mean it *wasn't that bad*? Of course it must be effing awful. It must have been, like, the living manifestation of the Third World in the First World.'

'No.' I was resolute in my conviction: 'My mother's work gave her a sense of purpose and dignity.'

'Dignity?' They were so wide-mouthed incredulous that I could see the masticated remnants of their beansprout alfalfa wholemeal rolls. 'What kind of dignity is that? That's exploitation!'

They wanted to see me as stoic, because they wanted to offer polite charges of bravery before charging on to their manifestos of destroying the capitalists. They needed a scapegoat, but I thought about my mother's 'friends' in the jewellery stores – the small-business owners: the Kims, the Trans, the Quachs – industrious people with terror in their eyes whenever they saw parking inspectors, let alone police. The university socialists needed to see me as a suffering victim who would stick with saying the mass line of over-throwing the whole exploitative system of labour. Instead, I became an employment lawyer.

At work, I visited sheltered workshops, places where people with severe disabilities were supported in the most simple of tasks: folding small paper boxes, sorting donated clothing, putting a cer-tain number of screws in containers. Some of the employees had worked there for more than four decades, doing the exact same thing day in and day out. The workshops were beautiful austere spaces, every corner cleaner and neater than our entire house in Braybrook. As I visited these places, Mum lay in bed without the disability pension because her physical disabilities weren't severe enough to warrant any compensation from anyone, and perhaps by the time they became severe enough she would have become too old to work anyway.

Now the shed no longer vibrates with its massive machine heartbeat. Red dust no longer floats out from beneath the door. But we are still not to speak of what Mum did for those two working decades of her life.

The door to the shed is still locked.

THROWING THE BOOK

The Old Man is sitting on a plastic chair outside the room, his hand resting on his wooden cane. His left leg cannot bend at the knee because an epoch ago the barefoot doctors in China gave him the wrong medicine for a minor foot injury. Now his leg sticks out in front of him and it looks as though he is trying to trip someone. He winces apologetically as people manoeuvre past. Some are pacing anxiously, fiddling with their clothes. Some are lolling wearily, as though they have been here many times before. None of them takes much notice of the Old Man.

The Uncle is here with his Niece. They came an hour early because they didn't want to be late. When the Uncle sees the Old Man, he calls out in Mandarin and walks over to greet him, careful to avoid the leg trap. 'Ay! Mr Zhang! Mr Zhang, so good to see you!' The Old Man nods and smiles.

You would think they were at a reunion. You would think they were old friends. In fact, they are about to battle it out with each other in the courts of the new country. More accurately, their advocates – the family members who speak English – are about to battle it out for them in the Victorian Civil and Administrative Appeals Tribunal.

'Case No. 54365 – Zhang v. Newtone Electronics,' someone calls out, and the Uncle recognises the name of his business. 'Ay,' he nudges the Niece, 'is that us? Are they calling for us?' The Niece nods, and the Uncle helps the Old Man to his feet while she hands him his walking stick. Together, they walk the Old Man to the room, lead him to the empty seat beside his Son-in-Law, and then take their places on the opposite side of the room. The Son-in-Law, a towering pink megaphone for his softly spoken in-laws, glowers at his wife: 'Doesn't your old man realise that they're the other side? Why's he getting so friendly with them?' The Old Man is silent, waiting for the hearing to begin.

'Just because they have a white son-in-law they think they can sue the hell out of us,' the Uncle told his Niece when he first appealed to her for help. 'Ungrateful Australians. Zhang bought that DVD player for his daughter. I know she and the white devil egged him on.' The Niece is a law student, in her second year. She has been practising law for her family members since she was sixteen: writing letters of complaint, deciphering employment contracts, submitting tenders. But this will be her first time in court.

Under the *Fair Trading Act 1999*, the fee to take a claim of less than $10,000 to the VCAT is $34.20. 'Such a small sum!' railed the Uncle when the VCAT notice first arrived. 'No wonder so many want their day in court.' For $34, anyone can experience Justice the democratic way. The Uncle believes this is why his Asian customers are so eager to take him to the tribunal. They are free, and by the blessed Buddha, they will sue each other for all it's worth. In a democracy, there is always someone to blame.

The Uncle shares their faith in this marvellous system. He knows that in this new country, everything is organised to be rational and fair and good, to remedy people who aren't. 'Do you think they would do this to a white man?' he exclaimed as they drove to the tribunal. 'Oh no, they would never try this at Harvey Norman. If the white guys at Myer tell them that they can't get a refund, then that's the end of the matter. But me, I'm just a Phnom Penh peasant, fresh off the boat – no harm in throwing a phonebook at *me.*'

Some disputes can be settled out of court. The day before the hearing, a different Chinese customer came into the Uncle's shop. Waving an ad from the local newspaper, he demanded the mobile phone in the window for $99.

'But that phone costs over $200,' implored the Uncle.

'Your ad says $99!'

'It says mobile phones *from* $99! I can't sell you that one for $99.'

'Ay, you shifty Chinese-Cambodians!' the customer shouted, picking up the Yellow Pages from the counter and lobbing it at the Uncle's head.

As the Uncle ducked, he recalled a passage from the franchise manual: *The customer is always right. Never lose your temper on the shop floor.* He picked up the phonebook, put it back on the counter and turned solicitously to the fuming customer.

'Go to Crazy John's,' he proffered. 'Go and throw something at him. Go and molest another Telstra dealer. We all have the same ad.'

The customer marched out, turning to have the last word before he left. 'You're lucky I don't take you to the tribunal!'

As they wait for the hearing to begin, the Niece reads over the documents once more. Question 11 asks the applicant to *Outline the history of the dispute. Attach extra sheets if you need more space.* Only five lines are provided on the form, but Mr Zhang's daughter has attached two extra pages of pain and suffering caused by the malfunctioning DVD player. Who can fit into five little lines their heart-rending history of corporate exploitation? You'd have to do it in haiku.

When the Tribunal Member enters the room, all stand up respectfully and turn to see what Justice looks like. He is a tired-looking man with greying hair. He sits at the front of the room, behind a raised desk, and signals wearily for them to sit down.

Standing up to speak for the Old Man, the Son-in-Law begins an indignant speech. The phrases 'dodgy goods', 'buggered up' and 'ripped off' occur several times, often in the same sentence. But the Tribunal Member cuts him off. He has witnessed this scene many times before; each tirade is identical to the last except for minor details of fact. The Member leafs through the application and sums up the two pages of woe in three sentences. Then, in shorthand, he states the law in relation to the matter, for the edification of all parties: 'The DVD player did not do what it was supposed to do – that is, play DVDs.'

It is the Niece's turn. She has studied Section 74D of the *Trade Practices Act*. She knows she has to prove that the DVD player was of merchantable quality when it was sold. She wants to explain that faulty discs inserted into the player might have caused it to malfunction. She also wants to point out that some DVD players can only play discs from certain zones. But when she stands up to speak, she finds that she has soaked up her parents' fear of authority. Her carefully rehearsed case comes out as two awkward sentences, speeding to a small smash of silence. This is not how she imagined her courtroom debut.

Her two pithy sentences have not convinced the Tribunal Member. He declares that the information is immaterial, and that the goods did not do what they were supposed to. Therefore the applicants are entitled to a full refund.

'But we offered four times to fix it for them because it was still under warranty!' exclaims the Uncle. 'But they would have none of it! You must tell him that the DVDs they were playing were *illegal*. How dare they sue us when they were breaking the law!'

The Niece begins to translate, but the Tribunal Member has

already made his decision. There are many other claims to be heard and judgements must be made quickly. A $34 fee does not warrant an hour-long stint in the judicial system. The parties stand up as the Tribunal Member walks out of the room.

When the Member has gone, the Uncle turns to the Old Man: 'We will write you a cheque.'

'Thank you.'

The Uncle answers in English, ignoring the smirking Son-in-Law: 'No worries.' The Old Man and the Uncle shake hands and give each other small pats on the back.

'I don't understand how we lost,' mutters the Uncle as they walk out of the building. 'The only reason the machine was not playing was because they jammed it up with a chopstick, trying to get a pirate DVD out. It was a good one too, a Panasonic.' The Uncle looks to the Niece for an explanation, for the complex legal reasoning behind the decision. All she can say is, 'The judge must not own a DVD player.'

'Don't worry,' says the Uncle, 'you did well. And Mr Zhang got his $34 worth – I guess it's true, the customer is always right. But all is not lost. We'll get the broken player fixed, hook it up to one of the display TVs and play the Tiger Soya-Milk Maker demonstration DVD on it.'

'Who'd want to buy a soya-milk maker?' asks the Niece sceptically.

'Ah. The Old Man,' says the Uncle. 'He'll come back to get one next week.'

'Do you really think he'll come back?' asks the Niece.

'Of course. Of course he'll come. He needs to collect his cheque. And you can't get one of those things from the white guys at Harvey Norman.'

HOME TRUTHS

Ah Gong is ninety-eight years old. Twenty years ago, he dug up his whole suburban backyard until it was only a field of soil. He built two rainwater tanks, and planted rows of vegetables – turnips, cabbages, onions – as well as an olive tree. Ten years ago, he was still farming his land. Ah Mah was twelve years younger. 'Old man,' she'd shout, because he was deaf in one ear, 'did you let loose on the carpet again?' But she always cleaned up after his stomach upsets. She also sewed all their clothes, right down to their underwear – heavy knitted polyester in dirt browns and navy blues and greys – until she couldn't anymore because of the arthritis. Sometimes they would fight. She'd take a hoe to his bok choy; in revenge, he'd hide the jar of Nescafé.

Two years ago, Ah Gong was sent to a nursing home. 'It's because you two fight too much,' his children told him, when it was really because they thought he was too frail to be in his garden. They'd tried having him in each of their homes, but were alarmed when they came home from work and discovered him outside, digging or trying to scale a stepladder, always itching to go back to his own land. He was almost deaf. He couldn't hear the phone. He was losing his sense of balance.

Ah Gong's children found him a light-filled nursing home in

an outer suburb, clean and bright, serving three-course meals that included mung-bean soup and jasmine tea. The website said that the home celebrated cultural diversity, but none of the carers could sing the Teochew opera he loved. Every Monday, a Filipino carer soulfully belted out classics like 'Morning Has Broken' and 'Over the Rainbow' to the assortment of Teochew, Hakka, Cambodian, Vietnamese, Cantonese and Hokkien residents arranged in a semi-circle in the living room. Another earnest carer danced and encouraged the residents to clap along, sometimes by taking their hands in hers. Some indignantly withdrew their limbs, some cheer-fully applauded, while others resigned themselves to being benign geriatric muppets.

The carers all call him Ah Gong, which means grandfather. They call another resident Bà, Vietnamese for grandmother. The carers might be 'Asian', but Asia is a big part of the world, so they could be Filipino, Taiwanese or Indonesian. Ah Gong can't speak English, and they can't speak his dialect. The European equivalent would be a home filled with Latvians, Slovenians and Moldovans attended to by Greek, Spanish and Irish nurses, doctors and carers. The staff are attentive but busy, solicitous but overworked.

'Boss, boss, why do you ignore me?' laments a Cantonese grandmother, to the departing back of a uniform. He could be Indian or Sri Lankan, she doesn't know the difference; and he doesn't realise she's speaking to him. She turns back to the baby doll she has in her arms, patting its soft limbs and plastic head with blinking long-lashed eyes, and cooing at it. Every evening at meal-time, a cheery woman comes to spoonfeed her mother a dinner she has prepared at home.

Ah Gong remembers, eighty years ago in China, how he slept away his days, emptied of energy and starving. The lucky ones never woke up. But one of his cousins had just returned from abroad.

That cousin saved his life, dragged his still-breathing skeleton onto a boat bound for Cambodia. He worked for a decade in the backs of kitchens, not knowing if he'd ever get married, until one day a friend said to him, 'I know a really good hard-working girl. Would you like to meet her?'

When Ah Mah also moves into the nursing home, the two are shifted to a twin room with a flat-screen television and an enormous ensuite. At meal time in the dining room, there is a feast in front of them: rice porridge, egg custard, leafy green soup, Chinese cups with lids to keep beverages warm, chopsticks and big plastic soup spoons. Wordlessly, Ah Gong hands Ah Mah a folded tissue from his shirt pocket. Ah Mah swaps her jasmine tea for his water.

Their granddaughter comes to visit, and Ah Mah laments, 'Oh, if only I had my rice cooker still, I would make dinner for you!'

'I can't recognise any of you now,' says Ah Gong, 'because none of you come and visit often! Tell your mum to take me home, or the only way I will be out of here is when I am dead on my back!' They'd never expected to grow old surrounded by strangers.

After the meal, a nurse comes by with tablets for each resident. Ah Gong and Ah Mah didn't take any medication before they moved to the home. Ah Mah refuses.

'What are these for?' asks their granddaughter.

'They're for her psychosis.'

'My grandmother doesn't have psychosis,' the granddaughter says. She knows her grandparents sequester food in drawers and cupboards until it rots, and are constantly searching for their 'missing' money, but most of the elderly former refugees she knows have these habits. Half a century ago, Ah Gong won a small local lottery and with his winnings brought home four durians for his wife and eight children. This was one of his life's highlights.

'Sorry, they're to help her sleep,' corrects the carer. 'She keeps getting up in the middle of the night and hurting herself.'

It is easier for the carers to look after this babel of old people if they are medicated, the granddaughter realises. They don't panic, or fight, or cry out in incomprehensible languages.

One night, Ah Mah has a stroke and is taken away.

'He doesn't realise she's gone,' says the carer with deep sympathy, a few days later, to the granddaughter. 'The family hasn't told him?'

They had been together for sixty-eight years and had never celebrated a single anniversary. They just got on with the business of surviving, day in, day out. His daughters tell him that they've taken Ah Mah to live with one of them.

'At least one of us made it out of here alive,' Ah Gong mutters.

When their granddaughter next visits, Ah Gong has packed his clothes in four large black garbage bags. 'Your aunties said they were coming to take me home,' he says, staring at the window. 'They visited this morning, and said they would be back this afternoon.'

It is a Monday afternoon, 3 pm, and the karaoke has started, but Ah Gong cannot hear a thing.

Hey, Jude, don't make it bad / Take a sad song and make it better.

RETURNING

About a year ago, my friend Suzanne went on Facebook to find our primary school buddies. Since I wasn't on Facebook, Suzanne showed me their profiles.

There was Danielle W., who had two kids, there was Timothy Z., who had two chins. There was Jack, Suzanne's primary school boyfriend, who had a $30,000 debt from his most recent divorce and now drove trucks for a living. There was Dang, whose mother and my grandmother had shared the same hospital room when I was sixteen, and when only one of them came home he still called me up, genuinely happy for us. There was Meghan, the star of the school play, still pretty; and Nathan, my best boy buddy in Grade Four, who was now openly gay in a suburb where that could mean a broken bottle-top to the face if you weren't careful.

'Remember her?' Suzanne asked me, clicking on an image of another very familiar face. Of course I did. She had been one of those happy-go-lucky, freckle-faced kids who smiled easily even when she lived off Vegemite sandwiches every lunchtime. Until our Facebook expedition, I had not thought about Layla Owen since primary school. Over the next week Suzanne told me she had been messaging Layla, and that we should pay her a visit. 'She has a kid now,' Suzanne told me, 'and doesn't go out much.'

So on a Friday evening after work, Suzanne drove us to visit Layla. We heard her before we saw her. A shadowy figure emerged from the front door of a concrete house in a suburb where most of the residents' blinds were drawn shut during the day, and where they took as much care of their homes as they did their teeth. She sounded like she was taking her first and last inhale and exhale with every breath, like someone was doling out limited free supplies of air the same way shopping-centre mall spruikers handed out chips in small plastic bags, and she wanted to grab as many as she could and use them all up before they expired.

She emerged a different shape and a different size from what we had remembered, as if someone had put her in the oven to rise, but she had still managed to retain her uncooked colour. As she came closer, even though her walk was different, and she was now an adult, we took a look at her face and realised that she still seemed exactly the same. That's the funny thing that happens with seeing someone you haven't seen in almost twenty years. They either look like the childhood version of themselves you have embedded in your mind, or they appear as complete strangers. But Layla was no stranger. In her face, we saw the familiar soft-pudding sweetness of an old friend.

'How have youse been?' She opened the wire-frame door for us.

'Yeah, not bad,' replied Suzanne. 'Same old.' When we entered, Layla's boyfriend was lying on the couch watching the footy. He just looked at us, and then back at the telly, like a walrus looking at some minor and unthreatening gyre in the ocean. Disinterested, uncurious.

Layla did not offer us food or a drink. This was not to be taken personally. All it meant was that she had never been taught that there was such an experience as 'having guests over'. I was familiar with this sort of thing. Growing up here, houses were not places where your friends' parents offered to share their welfare proceeds with others on a regular basis. Lining up at Kmart with my baby sister in a pram, sometimes you'd hear, 'Git lost, we were here first.' Minding my sister while she sat on the stationary plastic carousel horses at Highpoint that moved only when you put a dollar in, mothers would come with their kids and say, 'Git lost, we're not putting money in for youse too.' The baffling thing was that we never even *asked*. Yet those two sentences summed up life behind the carpet factories of Braybrook: *Git lost, we were here first*, and *git lost, we're not putting money in for youse too.*

Suzanne's father was a One Nation supporter who, after his divorce, solely dated small Asian women with minimal English skills. But when we were small he used to walk my brother and I home from school, take us to theatres and dole out countless kindnesses on us. Layla's mother came to my eleventh birthday party at McDonald's and gave me a doll. Their girls had grown into women, and they were still my friends, even though I knew their small talk would inevitably turn to a litany of complaints about the hardships of life and the crappiness of the government, despite their not being entirely sure whether the government we had was Labor or Liberal. It didn't matter, because the government was supposed to provide, and if it wasn't doing its job, then there was every right for the common citizen to bag them.

'Have you ever noticed the homeless in the streets?' Suzanne asked Layla. Just the other week we had been at Flinders Street Station at night, where Suzanne bought cheeseburgers for a woman who was sitting outside a McDonald's drawing chalk pictures on the footpath.

'Nah, I don't get out much,' replied Layla.

'Well, you'll notice one thing. They're all Australians.' Suzanne meant that they were all white. 'I think it's outrageous how our government can't even look after their own and yet are giving so much money for boat people and shit.'

Suzanne didn't realise what she was saying, because in her eyes I was like her. 'I swear, sometimes I forget that she's even Asian,' she once told a boyfriend, possibly the highest compliment you could offer in this area.

'Yeah,' Suzanne continued, 'I saw on the news that the government gives these people money to buy new cars and shit, when the rest of us are living rough, just trying to get by.' Centrelink wouldn't give you any money unless you had less than $3000 in the bank, something Suzanne had learnt the hard way one year when she lost her job at the glycerine factory.

'They don't even know how to drive,' decried Layla.

And suddenly I could see it from their perspective. What strange and grating feelings must have developed in their solar plexuses, these girls who had known only one way of life, to suddenly see an enormous swarm of crazy migrants in their neighbourhood who just worked day and night, and to see how hard they worked their kids, never taking a break until they had achieved the new car paid for in cash and not through a 24-months interest-free deal; the new house, mortgage-free after six years; and the new life away from the carpet factories. You weren't meant to pursue 'the Great Australian Dream', they had grown up believing. It was just an ideal, like a television advertisement, and class was as fixed as the fascinators on the heads of B-grade celebrities on Melbourne Cup Day. How did these outsiders cotton on to *how the system worked,* and how did they do in one generation what usually took two or three? There must have been something dodgy going on with the new arrivals. It was impossible to believe that you could come to a country with nothing and end up with more than everyone else. And yet it was not, when you considered how much they worked, these ethnic relentless pursuers of the Great Australian Dream. In fact, the amount of work they did seemed obscenely unAustralian.

*

So I learnt to make concessions, which were small concessions. I told myself, *you are skilled, you are university educated.* I chose to forget the blind panic that engulfed me in my mid teens, the fear of what would happen if I wasn't these things, if I was stuck, spending my whole life with the *git lost, we were here first* crowd. I reminded myself constantly *but for the Grace of God go I,* even though I wasn't Christian. How tenuous fate is, how largely due to luck. Anyone could be nice to symmetrical-faced, liberal-minded, healthy, vegetable-raised middle-class young women who said all the right things, but my friends were my friends because they were true and transparent: Layla, with her house decorated with Target Home Depot tables and Big W cushions. Suzanne, with her quiet grace, her carefully applied make-up and her clean shoes. They did not censor their views, they did not pretend to love when they felt fear, they did not pretend tolerance when they felt contempt. And as much as I disliked their ideas, we made a strange form of exceptionalism for each other. They were kind people at heart, they loved and tolerated others on an individual basis, even if *they* had 'Fuck off we're full' stickers on the backs of their cars. They had their strong views, but they were never going to be the policymakers, the teachers, the lawyers or the people in positions of power in this country, younger versions of which I encountered at university – people who would never let me get a word in, and who spoke with expertise about the Third World because they had visited Cambodia on a school trip when they were fifteen.

There was a little boy, about six years old, jumping on Layla's other couch. This was, I soon found out, Layla's son, Jayden. I told Layla how beautiful her son was, because it was true. I also knew that these people did not make conversation. They just muttered out loud, mental reminders directed at no one in particular: 'I gotta go to the dentist soon.'

'Oh yeah?'

Pregnancy had made Layla's teeth wobble, she told us, until she could almost move one of her front teeth at a forty-five degree angle. Eating felt like she had those fake pink-and-white lolly teeth in her mouth. And then, one day the teeth just started to fall out. So now she was waiting to get dentures made.

Jayden leapt onto the couch.

'Fucking git off me!' Those were the first words we heard the prostrate boyfriend say all evening.

Suzanne told Layla how we had, over the weekend, gone to a pub called the Sphinx in Geelong (the local residents referred to it as the Sphincter) to hear an '80s cover band called Shock Rock.

'Can youse come and pick me up when you have another one of those again?' Layla asked. She was almost pleading. She didn't have a car. 'I don't go out much, with Jayden and everything. And lazy shit here won't take me anywhere.'

'Fuck you.' Lazy Shit did not move from the couch.

'So can youse?'

'What are you going to do about your kid?'

'Lazy Shit'll look after him.'

I was inclined to be polite and say, 'Sure, when we next go we'll make sure to ask you along,' even though I had no intention of ever going back to see Shock Rock. But Suzanne didn't say anything, so neither did I. After all, I might have had the disingenuous good manners, but Suzanne was the one with the car.

'What does she do all day?' Suzanne wondered, after she pulled out of Layla's driveway. 'Imagine if we had never got out of the neighbourhood.'

We tried to.

But we couldn't. We didn't want to even think of the possibility. The evening was still young, too young to be tainted with such fears. We were driving away, and on the way back the lights were green in our favour.

STOP RACE MIXING!

When you are about seven months pregnant, you and your husband go to a local hardware store. When you return twenty minutes later to the car park, someone has put a folded piece of paper on your windscreen, held down by the wiper. You think it's just an advertisement, but when Nick unfolds it to take a look, he grows very agitated. 'I'm going to see if anyone else got this on their cars,' he tells you, and returns a few moments later. No one else has anything on their windscreen except youse.

You take the paper from him. At first it seems like a badly photocopied advertisement: a picture of a black boy and a white girl, both around ten years old, well-dressed, perhaps a promotional shot for an American '80s sitcom. The children are inside a circle, which you think is the frame of the picture, until you realise that the image inside is cut into quarters by a large thin cross. In capital letters on top of the picture are the words: STOP RACE MIXING. Then you realise – the kids are targets inside the barrel of a gun.

'Don't worry,' you say to your husband, 'I bet that STOP RACE MIXING person has a whole collection of posters he carries around, so when he sees men holding hands he probably pulls out his STOP GAY MARRIAGE and when he sees redheads eating bagels he takes out the STOP GINGER JEWS one.'

You find the incident harmless enough. Some cowardly moron is probably sitting in their car waiting to see your reaction. You imagine them grinning a nicotine-stained smile, smoking their taxpayer-funded cigarette and thinking, *Ha! That'll teach those miscegenating fornicators a lesson.*

When you tell your friends at the university college where you live and work, they are incredulously horrified and outraged. 'Clearly mentally ill,' they say. Or, a little self-righteously, 'Who are these people? They don't represent me or my country.'

But you know who these people are. Oh yes. STOP RACE MIXING and you go back a long way. When you were a sixteen-year-old sales assistant at your dad's electrical appliance store, old ladies would come in and say, 'Can I have an Australian salesman, thanks.' And you would dutifully go and find Joe the Italian or Jim the Macedonian.

When you are ten, Mum walks you home from school and sees a man mowing the lawn across the road. 'Go ask him how much he charges to cut grass,' she tells you. Mum speaks no English and the only literature she reads is the Kmart and BI-LO ads that come in your letterbox every Tuesday. You do as she asks. The man, older, with a face like beef jerky left out of the packet for too long, hollers at you: 'I DON'T DO YOUSE!' You report to Mum, 'He doesn't cut grass.'

'Of course he does, I've seen him doing the other lawns around here. Go back. He can't hear you through the lawnmower noise.'

You go back. He yells at you again. 'GIT LOST I DON'T DO YOUSE.'

You are mortified and ashamed, and at that moment you hate Beefjerk but also your mum for *not getting it.*

Your mum does not care if you are literate or not at school – her greatest fear is that soon you will not be able to speak to her in the same language. You, your brother and sisters already talk to one another in English. Your medieval dialect of Teochew cannot convey certain wonders, such as the pros and cons of each Teenage Mutant Ninja Turtle's powers and personality. So your parents sent youse off every week to learn a third language, one that can be an intermediary.

Mandarin school goes for only three hours every Saturday morning, with a half-hour break in between for recess. Because you are all grouped according to your oral and written abilities, there'd often be other fifteen-year-olds among the small mainland children, so you don't feel too out of place. And compared to real Chinese school for children in China, you are on a perpetual holiday. During the summer, you all bring along water balloons and in that hour drench one another so profusely that the last hour of class is hell for your poor, refined mainland teachers, who have to deal with a class full of wet, dripping, feral Western hoons.

During the school holidays, so many of youse fail to do your homework that the principal, Easter Wu, begins offering cash prizes to students who have. Two dollars for the best writing in class, and one dollar for the three runners up. 'Cheapskate Chinese,' mutters thirteen-year-old Corrina, the mongrel half-Australian in your class, and then she turns to the small seven-year-old next to her: 'Hey, kid, I'll give you a dollar if you say, "I don't wanna be a chinga!"'

James's eyes shine: he can spend hours copying the plotless stories in the textbooks written and sold by the principal, all about offering various fruit to your elders – *Grandma, eat this strawberry! Thank you, small child. Grandpa, have a banana! Here, let me peel it for you! Wah! What a good child.* – and making lovely accompanying illustrations of filial piety, or he can just take Corrina up on her offer.

'I don't wanna be a chinga!' grins James. 'Heh, heh.'

'Here you go, have a dollar.'

To those poor hardworking mainland Chinese teachers, Corrina probably represented a very good reason to STOP RACE MIXING.

*

You grow up with grandparents who survived the Chinese famine, uncles who survived the Cultural Revolution, a father who survived the killing fields of Cambodia and a mother who lived through the aftermath of the fall of Saigon, and you learn that to survive means to blend in, to try and render yourself invisible to any targets. You never know when the targets will change depending on the whim of political leaders, and you bide your time and wait for the aim of the gun to hopefully bypass you. When you were eight, someone chucked a rock through your window but your parents never got it repaired. Your mother just permanently lowered the blinds and quietly went about her work in the garage.

You grow up in a factory town that never recovered from the '80s recession. Vacant commission houses become a common sight along the streets of Braybrook, like a row of teeth rotting at an alarming rate. Old families move to more rural areas to find new jobs. Because rent is so cheap, new families begin migrating to this working-class neighbourhood that now has no work – Vietnamese, Tongans, Cambodians, mainland Chinese. But the new migrants are resourceful. They work as seasonal fruit-pickers, or in far-flung suburbs where other factories are running, or sewing in their poorly ventilated garages out the back. They don't mind spending four hours of their day on a bus. They don't mind eating instant noodles for two meals out of three each day. Some even save up enough to start small businesses.

Meanwhile, the factory closures reduce once-proud working-class white families to their second or third generation of welfare dependency. Like your own mother, the only literature these folks read are the supermarket ads, and the only news they see about yellow or brown people is on TV, on *A Current Affair*, about dodgy South-East Asian drug dealers, illegal immigrants coming here to steal their jobs and Indonesians locking up fun-loving Schapelle Corby. The other thing they watch on TV is *Neighbours*. In 1993 the first Asian family appears, the Lims from Hong Kong, who are then quickly accused of barbequeing a beloved neighbourhood dog.

But the old families in Braybrook barely see their Asian neighbours to know whether they cook family pets or not. Then, a decade later, they notice that those chingas have a new Toyota Camry parked in their driveway. When no one in their own families has ever owned a new car, and they're still putting advertisements in letterboxes to earn a buck, how come the government are helping refugees and not them? This is an outrage! The next day, after work, your dad notices that someone has made a deep angry scratch across the silver paint of his car boot.

*

A few years ago, you are in line at a shop in your home suburb. 'Here you go, sweetie,' says the sandy-haired woman behind the counter with the dangly triangle earrings, handing you your change and towels in a bag. You are still loitering at the store looking at discounted socks when you notice the next man at the counter. Dressed in the dignified two-decades-out-of-season suit of newly arrived migrants, he very politely asks for a bag. He'd bought polyester bedsheets in a slippery, clear plastic package. 'Nope,' says the woman definitively, 'we don't have any bags.' What she could have said was, *we don't have any big enough.* What she could have done, as other sales assistants had done, was offer to wrap two large bags together, or use string. But she doesn't.

And there it is – the moment you know that you are safe, that you have blended in so completely because there is a black Sudanese man behind you. The relief you feel, but also the guilt and pity – which is not a word we like using these days – towards the new arrival is enormous. You are now an invisible watcher, and your invisibility has come at the expense of someone else.

The man lowers his head, and then tries again. 'Sorry, I have to take this on the train. I cannot carry it like this. Please can you help?' This tall, regal man reduced to begging for two plastic bags. You cannot bear it. She throws them across the counter at him, and turns away to tidy up the till.

*

Years later, you are out of Braybrook and you have a job where the most dangerous workplace hazard is getting a papercut or scalding yourself with tea, not losing your forearm to a careless foreman in a factory. You get to write about your childhood and talk about race in public forums, and because you are in a position of comfort and respect, none of it seems so bad anymore. You can even laugh at STOP RACE MIXING while you are onstage with a barrister and a broadcaster at a writer's festival discussing Australia's national identity. The barrister says that the Australian identity has nothing to do with the Australian people, who are largely decent people: 'It is as if we live our lives simultaneous to these lives that the media project.' The broadcaster announces, 'Racism in Australia has a lot to do with class, and unless we address class difference, or our perceptions of the working class, xenophobia and racism will not change.'

We need to have these conversations about the shape of national identity, everyone concurs during the question-and-answer minutes allocated at the end of the panel. We need to start these conversations, as ordinary Australians, to show the world that we are not racist. But you know that back in Braybrook, no one is starting these conversations. There is a Burmese saying about not wasting your time playing a violin to a buffalo. To the people with whom you grew up, your working-class friends and family members, who has time to play a violin when the fields need ploughing?

*

You and your husband do not talk about STOP RACE MIXING except as a funny anecdote to share with others. These days, STOP RACE MIXING barely has any effect on you, because you are insulated by the kindness and decency of your new friends, many of whom have never even heard of Braybrook. No one except the mentally ill would be racist towards an employment rights lawyer who might help them with their unfair dismissal claim, they tell you. No one would be racist towards their Chinese family doctor. Woe to the poor sod who was dumb enough to put such crap on a writer's windscreen! This piece is going to be published, and you'll be paid for it. Meanwhile, STOP RACE MIXING may never get out of sordid suburbia, never have a voice beyond their self-funded poster campaign. Joke's on them, sucker! But in a way you know that you're also cowardly – STOP RACE MIXING and you are fighting a paper war, the only difference being that you have wider distribution.

Perhaps the truly brave are those who transcend the need to conduct The National Conversation, and go to direct action. Your Chinese school classmate Corrina would have hunted down

STOP RACE MIXING in the car park, taken down his number-plate, yelled out, 'Fuck you, inbred bogan', and later arranged for some of her boyfriend's homies to rearrange his/her car and/or face. No further words necessary.

LIVING WITH RACISM

In the killing fields of Cambodia, my father was threatened with having his tongue cut out with a sickle for speaking his native language, Teochew Chinese. When he and my pregnant mother arrived in Australia in 1980 and discovered that their new country encouraged them to maintain their language and culture, they were incredulous. My father named me Alice because he believed I was delivered into a wonderland, a place that allowed for the full expression of human personality and potential.

The White Australia policy, which barred non-white immigrants, had recently ended, and a new era of multiculturalism had begun. National policy mandated that at school we all learn another language in addition to English. There was an explosion of international food and festivals.

But Australia's fling with multiculturalism was temporary. In less than fifteen years, politicians began advocating assimilation for non-whites. In Australia today, the discussion around race and immigration has deteriorated to the point where many politicians no longer appear to believe that assimilation is even possible.

Racism has returned to the front of public discourse. Visiting Australia this week, the United Nations special rapporteur on racism, Mutuma Ruteere, condemned Australian politicians for 'xenophobic hate speech'.

I grew up near Footscray, a West Melbourne neighborhood then brimming with factories and optimism. Refugees had always moved to Footscray to start anew: Eastern Europeans in the 1950s and '60s, South-East Asians in the '70s and '80s, Africans in the '90s and the new century. A foreman gave my dad a trial at a car-trailer factory, thinking this 100-pound man would not be able to lift heavy metal parts. He didn't know that my father's previous job as a slave labourer was to bury dead bodies. He got the job.

But when businesses began to move production overseas in the early 1990s for cheaper labour costs, many proud working-class Anglo-Australians – including the kind of foreman who hired my father – were laid off. These were hard-working folks who had left school at fifteen and had been loyal to single companies for decades. The mood shifted. Some people in Footscray started to see multiculturalism as a punishment inflicted on them by the government. After all, it was the working-class whites who had to share their neighborhoods, jobs and schools with the new arrivals.

One evening, when my mother, brother and I were walking home, a car pulled alongside. The teenage passengers rolled down their windows and yelled out: 'Go home! Stop stealing our jobs!' I was too young to know that Australia was going through its worst recession since the Great Depression.

'Most Australians are good,' my father told us. 'Those are the bad ones. Just ignore them.'

My best friend's father mowed the lawns at our school. Her mother worked for the juvenile justice department. They were white Australians who lived in a concrete house like ours. The mother would tell us about poor children she encountered who felt hopeless; one kid was so desperate he injected Vegemite in his veins in search of a high.

Unlike their fathers and grandfathers, these working-class white kids could no longer leave school at fifteen and easily find jobs that would set them up for life. Now they were lost, on the streets causing trouble, tormenting the newcomers. The immigrants were also scrabbling at the bottom of the barrel, yet we were seen as the main threat to the Australian working-class way of life.

It had long been this way for migrants in Australia. In drafting the *Immigration Restriction Act* of 1901, Alfred Deakin, who later became prime minister, specifically went after Asian immigrants. 'It is not the bad qualities but the good qualities of these alien races that make them so dangerous to us,' he said. 'It is their inexhaustible energy, their power of applying themselves to new tasks, their endurance and low standard of living that make them such competitors.'

In the mid-1990s, Pauline Hanson was elected to parliament and formed her new political party One Nation, claiming that Australia was in danger of being 'swamped by Asians'. It was an easy claim to make: in 1971, the Asian population of Footscray made up a mere 1 per cent of the population, but by 1996, it had risen to 17 per cent.

At the same time that Dad was telling us to ignore the Bad White Australians, Bad Asians were beginning to appear everywhere. Vietnamese heroin dealers on the seven o'clock news, Filipino welfare cheats on the radio, Chinese slumlords in the papers. Ms Hanson declared that Asians had 'their own culture and religion, form ghettos and do not assimilate'. People started wearing printed yellow t-shirts, the word 'full' emblazoned across a map of Australia.

Keep your head down, my parents advised, because there was no point in fighting such bigotry.

The next time I went to my best friend's house, her father had tacked up a poster of Ms Hanson draped in the Australian flag. He sought to reassure me that it had nothing to do with our family. Echoing my father's line about white Australians, he said, 'Youse are the good ones.'

After almost two decades out of parliament and a brief stint in jail, Pauline Hanson has been re-elected to the Senate, her One Nation party winning four seats there. Now their main target is Muslims, but the game is the same.

As Mr Ruteere, the UN official, pointed out, our problems in Australia are not unique; in Europe and America similar xenophobic ideologies are brewing. Refugees are no longer comforted by a welcoming Australian government. Our new arrivals are no longer benefiting from a national policy of multiculturalism that tells them they belong. They are told to fit in or get lost, yet no one demonstrates how to achieve this assimilation.

I now understand how terrified those without power in Australia feel. I am reminded of a line in Ecclesiastes: 'I saw the tears of the oppressed and that they had no one to comfort them. On the side of their oppressors was power, but they had no one to comfort them.'

Racists feel that no one, neither society nor the government, appreciates how the modern world has left them behind. But one group shares their unrelenting feelings of deep-seated fear and anxiety: their victims.

What I have learnt from experience is this: in your moments of vulnerability, the bigots will still come for you. Your tongue could still be cut out, your windows smashed. You can go about quietly achieving and trying to keep a low profile, but you can never choose invisibility. When the bigots decide to see you, they will see you.

But I am no longer keeping my head down. I can see them, too.

WHO IS THE ORDINARY REASONABLE PERSON?

Senator the Hon. George Brandis QC
Attorney-General, Minister for the Arts
Parliament House, Canberra

Dear Senator Brandis,

According to your proposed amendments to the *Racial Discrimination Act 1975*, the standards of 'ordinary reasonable members of the Australian community' will determine whether or not something is 'reasonably likely to vilify' a particular race, colour, nationality or ethnicity. If I may, please let me introduce you to three candidates for your cohort of 'ordinary reasonable members of the Australian community'.

It is just after midday in the back room of an electrical appliance store, and these men are having lunch. They are retail veterans, having done the same job for at least two decades: the guy from the warehouse who has hands like leather gloves and can dismantle a fridge box in a few minutes, the fast-talking guy from the shop floor who's planning his once-in-a-lifetime holiday to Europe, and the manager who likes to put heartfelt homages to Steve Irwin in his shop ads. But business isn't so good these days. The store is in one of the most archaic and faltering of commercial places, a shopping strip. Down the same street are a Mediterranean restaurant, an African hairdresser, a Vietnamese chemist. Around the corner there used to be an adult video store next door to a halal butcher and an optometrist.

The manager and the warehouse man lean over the salesman, who is holding an open newspaper. Reading this particular paper is a sign of cultural belonging and a protection against the hostile world outside. 'Look at this,' the salesman says, referring to the sentiments expressed on their favourite columnist's page. 'The government says no to racism, but yes to free speech.'

The manager knows all about this freedom of speech. In his previous life, some soldiers once caught him speaking his own language to another man. The two men were made to kneel down and stick out their tongues, while the soldiers – young boys, really – wielded sickles to inflict a medieval punishment. The men begged their way out, but the manager will never forget such terrorism. Luckily, that kind of thing doesn't happen in this country. They've all come here for safety.

In his younger days, the warehouse man once saw a truck that was loaded with starved bodies on their way to burial. 'Some of their limbs were still moving!' he said, shaking his head. They vote for the party that will give each man and his family a sense of security.

The proposed amendments to the *Racial Discrimination Act* say that whether something racially vilifies or intimidates will not be determined 'by the standards of any particular group within the Australian community'. This neighbourhood is a place where 'no particular group' resides, so maybe these lunchroom guys are the 'ordinary reasonable members of the Australian community' on whose views this judgement will be based. I certainly hope so, because one of them is my father.

The people in my father's shop have come from places like the former Yugoslavia, the south of Italy, Vietnam, Cambodia and India, and they have escaped communism, socialism, ethnic cleansing, anti-Semitism, war and hunger. They see themselves as real men, not wusses with easily 'hurt feelings'. They know that one day the talk will come back to them again. How they should not be in this country if they are ungrateful. How they should not be here if they continue to speak their own language, if they don't assimilate.

These guys may have to look up the word 'bigot' in a dictionary, yet they understand racism on a visceral level. In their sixth or seventh decade of life, they sigh and know nothing has changed about human nature or racism but at least laws in Australia protect them from getting killed or bashed.

'Australian newspapers are not like the ones back home,' Dad tells me. 'They would never publish anything untrue.' These men know they'll never be in the paper unless they do something dodgy, and that's fine. Their hope is for their kids to be better educated and to have a voice.

My university studies and legal work taught me how to engage in reasoned debate, just as yours did, Senator Brandis. Yet I take no comfort in the fact that I may belong in your 'reasonable member' group that determines standards, because the problem with my voice is this: I have never known what it is like to be denied housing or jobs because of my race, to be dragged away by soldiers in the middle of the night, to be forcibly separated from loved ones or have my land pilfered. If someone yells abuse at Salesman Charlie, Warehouse Jack or my dad, if someone clenches their fist at one of these guys because of their skin or language or food, these men think there will be a knock on the door, their houses will be burnt down, their tongues cut off, bodies carted away in trucks, accented sons bashed up in the street.

The sort of fear that exists in their minds might lead a more 'reasonable' person to wonder: *Why are you carrying on like Armageddon will come? Why can't you form a decent coherent sentence? You can't even let go of past grievances and move on, you behave irrationally, and for crying out loud, speak English on a bus!*

Under the proposed amendments, these reactive, inarticulate, overly emotional 'feeling' types will suddenly not be reasonable persons by any stretch of the law. Fear is not an abstract thing debated by politicians, Senator Brandis. These folks see fear where no one else does: in public transport inspectors even though you bought a train ticket, in realising you have too many soccer mates walking down the street at the same time because you're all black, in always having a light on in the house even when you sleep.

If Dad and his mates stick up for one another when they feel vilified or intimidated, will they be regarded as 'sticking up for their own', considering that their neighbourhood is often written up in the media as an 'ethnic' enclave?

While you were studying law and politics as a young man, Pol Pot's bigotry led directly to the deaths of half our extended family in Cambodia. Imagine if you had been assigned the task of burying the bodies of your starved loved ones in a mass grave – as my dad had to do – and you might want to reconsider whether it is wise to give those with the loudest media voices the right and liberty to be 'bigots'.

It is 12.40 and lunch is ending. 'Of course we're reasonable,' my father concludes, and the lunchroom supports him. These folk have more faith and trust in Australian democracy and the media than any flag-waving patriot. 'Of course they're going to judge it by the ordinary individual, and not the terrorist extremist or the sort that has their head stuck in books.'

MUM IN THE FORBIDDEN CITY

THE WINTER AFTER
THE OLYMPICS

Beijing after the Olympics was one long exhale of cooling winter air. I had deliberately come to this city after the festivities, because I wanted to feel the heartbeat of the country when it was working and resting, not decked out and dancing. As the days grew shorter, I stayed indoors for greater stretches of time. I was living in a flat in Peking University as the 2008 Asialink writer-in-residence, and to alleviate my bouts of loneliness I would often go on long walks and watch people.

Romance did not seem to be openly slathered about in salacious glory on the streets. I barely saw any public kissing or embracing, but I watched old men and women linked arm-in-arm hobbling down the roads, their green and brown padded army coats blending in with the tattered winter trees. Although they needed to lean on each other for support, they seemed as firmly grounded as their ancient avenues.

One evening, I unexpectedly came upon the scene of a large crowd of old people dancing in a public square in the Hou Hai district, to the sound of loudspeakers. Hou Hai means 'the Back of the Sea'. It used to be an area filled with unassuming geriatric living, before the bars crammed themselves in the streets like contesting cancan dancers. The bars now line the area, leaving a space of concrete square for the old people to conduct their public lives. While the young rammed themselves inside expensive wine establishments and claustrophobic nightclubs, these old people did it all outside for free. The first time I saw it I was so moved I became teary, for a reason I didn't understand.

When I watched them closely, I realised the reason they danced like awkward schoolchildren was that their bones could not bend all that far. These were people who had toiled together through the decades, through the Cultural Revolution, through austere times. This bright Beijing of shining steel was beyond some of their wildest imaginings, but they had stayed together through all the unglamorous, severe years and could still come out and dance at night.

I arrived in this city on Bare Branches Day, called this because the date 11/11 resembles bare branches, the Chinese term for singles. I read a *China Daily* newspaper article which told me that by 2020 there would be a surplus of 30 million men of marriageable age in China. However, Beijing is the Chinese city with the most single women per capita. A sociologist in the paper was quoted as saying that 'while women look for better educated men with higher pay and social status, men prefer their partners to be young and pretty'. I didn't need a sociologist to tell me this, as I glanced at the people walking towards the clubs, digital cameras swinging at their wrists.

I looked back to my old dancers – these people didn't bring cameras. These were people who had probably never worn make-up in their lives, but on their faces were the lines of experience and love. They were one another's mirrors. And I wondered why we were so obsessed with our own faces when we didn't see them most of the time anyway – we see the faces of others. I watched the young people just down the road buy expensive sweet-nothings for each other – t-shirts that flashed with battery-operated lights, pink mink earmuffs and dangling doodads for their mobile phones. *Hao wanr* seemed to be the catchphrase of the modern youth – how fun! It was advertised on television everywhere, alongside creams for whitening one's skin. At every pause, there must be a photograph taken on a digital camera to capture the moment. Desire runs rampant on designer shoes, and an entire generation is rendered invisible by the new youth who need to see themselves to know that they exist.

In this fast world, I also felt unsophisticated, particularly in my waterproof parka and bush tracker boots. But just as long as my basic needs were met, I could take myself back and quietly observe. Despite years of attending Chinese school in Australia, I discovered how little Mandarin I could speak, and, accordingly how little 'personality' I had. All my moods and thoughts were reduced to the simplest of expressions – happy, sad, excited, tired, full. There were nuances of temporary feeling, of course – anxious, wistful, pleasantly surprised – but I felt no particular need to share them or solidify them. There was no desire to assert my sense of capital 'I' identity in this country that had the good grace of assuming I was one of its own by virtue of the way I looked.

Both sets of my grandparents were born in Guangdong state, China. But famine early last century forced them to take a boat to Cambodia, where my parents were born. When the dictator Pol Pot took over Cambodia, my father's job during the four years of that genocidal regime was to make fertiliser and bury dead bodies. When he arrived in Australia as a refugee, he never looked back.

I took a trip to Jie Yang and Puling, the birthplaces of my grandparents. The first of three generations to go back to our ancestral homeland, I rode an overnight train to Guangzhou, and then my friend Peina took me to Jie Yang on a bus. When I stepped off the bus onto the soil of Jie Yang, there was a Mcdonald's at one end of the city, and loudspeakers blaring out the Black Eyed Peas in front of franchise clothing stores at the other. A rickshaw driver pulled up in front of us and asked if we wanted a tour of the town. 'The surrounding areas,' Peina said, aware that I was a foreigner who would want to see the temples and far-flung places.

Over the decades my grandmother had told me the story of her small village in China, and when I arrived in the beautiful sprawling metropolis of Jie Yang, I realised that home was not a place but a people, and once the people were gone, then your sense of identifying with the land was also gone. An older person was my connection to history. It was as simple as that. And once that person was no longer around, no longer alive, they could not bring the world back for me. I felt no more pride that my distant, distant ancestors built the temple of Heaven than I did that the French created the Louvre. These things were the pinnacle of human achievement, but they did not belong to a particular lineage. Art was never intended to be exclusive. It seemed to be the very reason why the Forbidden City was opened up for the people. I could not claim this city as mine. I would never be the sort of tourist who could say 'I did China' or 'I did Cambodia', because these places are so much of my heritage that it would sound neo-colonial.

As the rickshaw driver drove us out of the city and into tiny village streets, I noticed the children. Some of them were in school uniforms – practical tracksuits in primary colours – while others were in pyjamas. They loitered around their parents' shop fronts, they chased chickens, and they pulled smaller siblings and cousins around in wooden barrows.

Suddenly I understood the moiling mentality of my parents, the race of small-shop-owners who took boats out of the south of China to South-East Asian countries – Vietnam, Thailand, Laos, Cambodia, Indonesia. The overseas Chinese, the *Huaqiao*, the class of small industrious merchants that made their livelihoods from trade. Looking at this life in a village halfway across the world and beyond three generations, I realised that these values formed a large part of my heritage in Australia. The staying at home looking after younger siblings in a suburb filled with factories. The hanging around my father's electronics shop after school every day and helping to sell toasters, heaters and blenders. These small communities that were accused of 'forming ghettos and not assimilating' were just replicating life as they knew it two generations ago.

When I headed back to Beijing, with its skyscrapers and factories and chimneys like upright cigarettes against the sky, I realised how different it was from the south of China. Beijing was the sophisticated capital. If she were a woman, she'd be tall, cultured and decked out in winter furs. I went back to sitting in local parks in my parka and bush tracker boots, and watching the retired older people amble past.

In every park I saw what looked like children's play equipment. But then I noticed that unlike the children of Jie Yang, who just hung loose in the smaller villages like scattered marbles, the city children all seemed to play indoors. The colourful bits of metal were actually outdoor exercise equipment for the elderly, to keep their bodies healthy.

I watched an old woman bending her knees on a nifty metal contraption consisting of two steps powered by arm levers. I saw a girl holding her mother's handbag as her mother had a go on the outdoor back-massager. And then I saw him, an old man flipping himself around and around a bar raised from the ground – more agile than a twenty-year-old – and I knew I was witnessing China's soaring rise, her verve for life embodied in this unassuming seventy-year-old acrobat swinging in the air, and yet so grounded in the moment.

MUM IN THE
FORBIDDEN CITY

Mum arrived in China decked out in gold. She had gold in little bags in her big bag. She even wore the gold Citizen watch we bought her three years ago for her birthday. It didn't matter that the watch was no longer ticking. She wore all the jewellery she never wore in the normal daily life of lifting boxes and selling washing machines and toasters at the electrical appliance store where she was a saleswoman. We had never seen Mum wear so much jewellery.

When I was sixteen, Mum decked me out in gold too. She filled my pockets with it, but warned me never to flash it around. Every couple of weeks, Mum would need me to do deliveries in the city. She had dozens of rings with tiny, grasping claws, and she needed the Lebanese man in the city to drill cubic zirconias and sometimes diamonds into them. Mum asked me to go because it was more convenient; my school was a tram ride away from Swanston Street.

Century Building was one of those hidden multi-storeyed old office buildings that had once been someplace quite swish, because the floor of the foyer was still tiled with careful regal-looking mosaics in heritage reds and whites. On level five there was a little gold-smithing business owned by two young Lebanese brothers or cousins. I would press the buzzer outside their door, because they had installed a buzzer after a recent shoot-out in the building.

'Who is it?' one of them would ask.

'I have a delivery from my mother.'

I would hear the buzzer sound like an insect in its death throes, and then I would be let in.

I would hand over the small bag of twenty-four-carat rings and pendants to one of the brothers-cousins. 'Come back next week,' they would tell me. A week or two later, I would go back to collect the goods and pay for the services. Mum told me to count the rings and pendants carefully before I handed over any money, so I did a careful count. But I barely glanced at the rings except to see that the stones were in place. I did not feel twenty-four carat. I still wore socks from Forges and a primary-school boy's shirt beneath my blazer at school, and didn't care. I also did not tell any friends at school. What could I say? 'My inner blazer pocket is filled with a thousand bucks worth of twenty-four-carat gold'? Diamonds were not my best friend, especially when I had to go through the whole school day scared shitless about losing them. Sometimes I would also go to Century Building to buy goat's hair brushes for Mum – she used them to polish off the gold – or a kilo of silver when silver was having a good price on the stock market. And jew-ellery boxes, because Mum would give away some of her creations as gifts at Chinese weddings, to the bride and groom.

In return for my gold-smuggling at school all those years ago, Mum helped me smuggle seven copies of my book into China in her suitcases, so I could give them to friends and professors. A box had been sent by my publishers, but they'd never seemed to reach their destination. In Mum's suitcase were also thirty boxes of choco-late seashells, to give to people who had been kind to me over the past three months. And Dad's small deliveries of love – Cadbury chocolate blocks doubly-wrapped over with Glad Wrap. Oil of Olay.

My sister Alison brought along a near-empty suitcase, because I told her we would need to buy a lot of winter coats. They were cheap here, and we should stock up on them like we stocked up on toilet paper. I also needed her to help me bring some inappropriate clothes home from China. Before I arrived in Beijing I was told it was cold. So while I was living in Wagga Wagga, I had bought a ski jacket and ski pants. I thought I would wear them in public. I ended up wearing them for days on end when I was sequestered alone in my flat, inadvertently detoxing on complimentary Peking University jasmine tea and writing about people who froze to death during winter.

Mum woke up at seven every morning while Alison and I slept in. We were just lazy. Mum pottered around, and ate breakfast (two-minute noodles). She would not go out alone, or explore or ask for things, even though she could speak the language better than the two of us combined. She needed us as her clutch. She had no independence because she'd had no friends for two and a half decades. But then she would also blurt things out like, 'I will never go on holidays with any of you again!' At first taken aback by the abruptness of these declarations and the frequency at which they came, I quickly remembered that this was just Mum's manner of speaking.

Mum had blood pressure tablets in her bag. I discovered them on the first evening she arrived, because she asked me for a cup of water.

'Why are you taking these tablets, Ma?' I asked.

'Why does it look like?' Her blood pressure was ridiculously high, Alison told me. Alison would know, because Alison had become a medical student. It was strange — how this little sister who'd once dressed up as a white puppy for a book parade in Grade Four had suddenly materialised into a medical student who could take my blood pressure and tell me about all the bones in the human hand.

All Mum seemed to want to buy was underwear and socks in China, from the Chinese equivalent of our two-dollar stores, except in the ones in China all the goods were coated with a light talcum of pollution-dust. Then I realised that I had been doing the same for the past two and a half months – I would go to these places to get rolls of sticky-tape, coloured paper, yellowy envelopes that could not be licked unless you believed in voluntary euthanasia.

Mum looked at the Beijing women in the city and realised they were dressed so well that we looked like peasants. So she took us to the Zoo Market and pointed out clothes we could get. Funnily enough, even though Mum was a dag herself, she could pick out the really trendy-looking clothes for us. When I first started working as a lawyer, I went to Footscray to buy two serious-looking austere suits. The rest of my wardrobe materialised over the course of two years – Mum would go to the sales at Myer and pick out the best silk shirts, the most sophisticated jackets with their tucks and pleats, the colours so subtle and elegant it was as if she knew the colour coordinates of the Myer catalogues inside out.

Every few months or so when I went home, Mum would tell me, 'Ay, I was in the Myer sales and I found a good work shirt for you.'

'You really shouldn't have, I have too many clothes already.'

'You can't just keep wearing the two daggy suits forever!'

One thing I learnt to appreciate about my mother was her frankness in her thoughts. Perhaps only educated white people got political correctness; they were the ones who made the whole concept up. I noticed this with my aunty from Hong Kong, when we went to the Lantau Buddha. There was a black father with his little girl. 'Wah!' exclaimed my auntie. 'Look at that little girl's hair in all those plaits. How pretty. She must be about twelve? What a big bum she has. Black children have nice round booty.'

Mum was the same. When she first saw me, she exclaimed over the phone back home to Dad about me: 'Lucky she still has teeth, otherwise her face would cave in and she would look like a grandma!' True, I was not glowing like roses, and the pollution sickness was taking its toll after three months, but my face was not an inverted Mount Vesuvius either.

My mum met my friends in Beijing – all of them were girls about four or five years younger than me, from different regional provinces. Their names were an assortment of repeated syllables: Ying Ying, Lily, Wawa, Ping Ping and Pan Pan, which meant 'Fatty'. They wore Converse sneakers that were exact copies of the originals but a quarter of the price, and their shoes were still white or pastel pink after three years because they cleaned them carefully with old toothbrushes.

Suddenly, our class elevation became evident – the Lancôme creams, the leather handbags from Italy that Dad bought home from his trips but Mum never used. Clothes bought on sale from Myer, and shoes bought on sale from Target. She was proud of their Australianness, and our friends were awed by our element of the overseas. If only they knew that our ordinary lives were made up of so many Made in China products.

I had done things here within my three months. I had exchanged money, opened a bank account, quickly worked my way around the public transport system and the subways. It was strange to sign a contract opening a bank account without being able to read the terms and conditions. 'Now you know what a torment it is not to be able to read,' Mum told me.

Before Mum had arrived, I had just let things languish. I didn't dare ask for too much. Funny how refugees demanded so much of their world, but as a hotel guest, with every accompanying status and privilege, I felt I could not inconvenience others. Meals were reduced to the lowest common denominator. I did not know there was a microwave just a few metres down the hall, a kitchen with boiling water, a cooktop. I had been there almost three months. I never ventured down the dark corridor, never knew who my neighbours were. I would go to the cafeteria with my meal card and point at the food I could see. I could understand what people said to me, but it was easy to get by without speaking many words.

We didn't think that the same rule applied to our parents, particularly not my mum, in this country filled with people who spoke Mandarin. She spoke three different forms of Chinese, Vietnamese, and Khmer. Five languages in all – so when we stood outside the Forbidden City, we thought she would naturally be able to lead us in.

'What does the sign say, Mum?' we asked. 'How much does it cost to get in?'

She remained silent. She was concentrating.

I glanced up and saw that the ticket prices were in English as well as Chinese. It took a couple of seconds for me to figure out how much it would cost for two adults and a student. I waited for my mother, who was reading the Chinese sign. It had no numbers on it, and I noticed her eyes stopping at each word, squinting. It was then that it hit me – that reading Chinese ached her eyeballs as much as looking at English, which for her was entirely indecipherable.

'I think it's forty kuai for all of us to get in,' I said, and lined up to buy the tickets. I didn't think she heard me. She was still standing there, looking at the sign.

I came back with the tickets, and Mum looked a bit bewildered. The world was just too difficult to read, and you had to rely on people all the time.

We went in.

We were inside the Forbidden City, the world's largest surviving palace compound, made of precious Phoebe zhennan wood sourced from the jungles of south-western China, and large blocks of marble sourced from quarries near Beijing, and paved with polished 'golden bricks' from Suzhou. The only non-castrated male in the place for hundreds of years had been the Emperor. Five hundred concubines to service one royal prick, and hundreds more eunuchs to wait on these ladies of leisure. Eunuchs swapped their reproductive organs for a hope of exclusive access to the Emperor, who made some into rich and influential politicians. Their *bao* treasure, their severed genitals, were kept pickled in a jar so they could be buried as complete men.

I looked into one of the Emperor's bedchambers. A place once lavished with swishy embroidered silk sheets, the bed made of wood that glowed. I had read that the Emperor would choose a concubine on the advice of astronomers. Four eunuchs would then deliver her to his bedchambers, rolled in a blanket like a gift waiting to be unwrapped. To make sure she concealed no weapons, she would be buck naked beneath.

'Don't look in there,' said Mum, 'it's dark and dirty.'

Suddenly, after Mum's words, I saw the immediacy of the moment: it *was* dark and dirty, poorly-lit and -ventilated, and felt as preserved as dried eunuch balls tied with string. History seemed only for the literates. Those who find it hard to look at words see an old building blocked off from public access with dust gathering in the corners of the darkened rooms.

I decided to take Mum and Alison to the Hall of Clocks, the pièce de résistance of the whole tour. You didn't need signs to tell you how ineffable these feats of engineering were. But Mum, who was a fifty-year-old, was behaving simultaneously like someone seven and someone seventy. She had no tolerance for walking long distances, she said; but the other day we had spent half a day trawling through bright malls. I had to coax her to keep going.

About fifty metres before the Hall of Clocks, she suddenly stopped and yelled, 'I am not going any further! You are going to kill me!' She was so loud and abrupt that some people stopped to look.

Mum went over to a bench and sat down.

'Would you like some food?' I asked her.

She did not reply.

'Are you tired? Would you like to go home?'

'Aiyoh, taking me to these places to kill me!' she yelled.

'Let's go back and have a rest then. I will get a taxi.'

'Wasting money again!'

I didn't know what to do.

Most nights while Mum and Alison were in Beijing, I lay awake, riddled with bullet holes of anxiety. Never in my adult life had I spent so much uninterrupted time in the company of my mother – two whole weeks, living in my small apartment at Peking University. Growing up, we had been in the same house together, and Mum and I had even worked in the same room, but we barely spent any time together because that was something people who weren't constantly working did. A few years ago I had taken her to Adelaide, when I was there for a few days for a writing festival. We spent a lot of time riding the free bus around and around the city, and Mum just talked to me. That was the first time I realised the meaning of quality time, and how proud my mother was of me.

But this time was different.

This time Mum felt old and lost, which made her angry. 'I will never go on holidays with any of you again!' she yelled.

We all sat on the bench, quiet and miserable, without knowing fully why. I'm not sure Mum knew either.

Suddenly, in front of us stood a man in a yellow cap.

'How are you, young ladies?' he asked in Mandarin. 'Would you like to go on a trip to visit four different Beijing landmarks in one day?'

He was an illegal spruiker who was standing around promising day trips on the bus to four different places for under fifty kuai. I thought Mum would tell him to go away, because it was obvious that he shouldn't have been there. But her head shot up and she looked interested. 'What are the places?'

'The Ming Tombs. The Sacred Way. Then the Birds Nest and the Water Cube. On the way back we might drive around past the CCTV tower too.'

There was no way that this tour could cover all those places unless they stayed on the tour bus the whole time, I thought.

But perhaps that was the point.

Mum said yes to the tour. She was going to go with Alison, while I had some work to do in my flat.

The next day, as promised, the tourist bus arrived at 6 am to collect them from the university. I got a call on my mobile, and passed it on to Mum. Because it was winter, the sky was still dark outside.

'Why have you come so early?' she asked. 'You said that you would come at eight.' I couldn't hear what was being said on the other end of the line.

Mum turned to me. 'What do you think?' she asked. 'Should we go or not?'

'Why did they come so early?' I asked.

'They said that they have other people to pick up along the way.'

'Two hours to pick up other people?' It seemed a bit suss to me.

'I don't want to go,' said Alison, who just wanted to go back to bed and sleep until daylight appeared.

Mum decided that it was too dangerous to go, and they stayed inside instead.

Mum met my professors in Beijing. Professor Hu invited us to lunch at a Shanghai restaurant, and Alison and I sat there in silence while Mum and the professor chatted. I realised something that I had not known before, listening to her speak – I realised that my mother was funny and endearing in her honesty.

'We were about to board a bus, Professor, to go on one of these tours. Because it was advertised at fifty kuai a person, to see about six places in one day. Wah! What a bargain! I thought. Then they called my mobile phone at six in the morning and said they were waiting at the front of the university for us. The sky was still dark! I was thinking, wah! What if they drove us off and then dumped us halfway, demanding more money?'

She had a quality of earnestness about her, and of direct confiding truth. She had not had the requisite experience with these sorts of educated eminents to realise appropriate situational anxiety, so she carried none. 'Aiyoh, I am so worried, Professor. My daughter is going to be thirty soon and still unattached.' She asked the professor to find a suitable student for me. Professor Hu looked at me and chuckled. He then told Mum a story about how he had set up two of his students. He concluded by saying, 'But these two students – I had known them for years, so I knew their temperaments and their interests. But these days, I think young people like to choose for themselves. They don't want an old grandpa making the most important relationship in their life for them.'

'But Professor, she is getting old. I don't mean to set them up – but if you know anyone . . .'

I realised that ten years ago I would have been furious with this. But I just looked at Alison with a jovial glint in my eye, and she gave me a half smile. Mum was funny. And this realisation was followed by a sudden stab of sadness. Our mother was growing old, but so were we. Back then, the world had seemed so small and confined – from her tin work shed to the house, from the house to Dad's shop. Two decades and four children later, she was in China with us. We had wanted her to see the world at large and marvel over it as we had in the Hall of Clocks, to taste real Peking duck, to stand on the Great Wall and take in the stretch ahead with a slow and long exhale. But she seemed happy enough not to exercise her peripheral vision. Perhaps she knew she wouldn't have been able to recognise any symbols and signs of this sweeping, baffling culture if they'd suddenly appeared; and anyway, it was only us, her children, that she wanted within her line of sight.

SEARCHING FOR AI HUA
IN AMERICA

In a far-flung corner of the world, I had been asked to search for my mother's childhood friend. And she was still unmarried, my mother added in an eye-widening, voice-quietening manner, as if she were saying that her friend had leprosy or cancer. 'That girl was always too stupidly generous,' my mother sighed, 'she always kept giving things away, and paying for things for other people. Her father died when she was young.' My mother paused. 'She had a suitor once, who wanted to take her abroad. But the mother didn't want her daughter to leave her all alone in her old age.'

This was the first time I'd heard of the ones who'd chosen to stay behind. My mother's best friend, back then, would have probably been in her mid-twenties, knowing that if she couldn't set sail with her lover, then she would miss both her boats. But she stayed in Saigon after the war.

For my mother, friends were memories from childhood and young adulthood. Once in Australia, she no longer had any more friends. Friends were to while away idle time with, and my mother had no more idle time. All she seemed to do was sequester herself in the garage, working at her jewellery trade, chipping away at the decades with her peeling tools and peeled hands. After a while, work became more fulfilling than the strain of watching people's moods.

As much as she tried to lock them into her mind as fixed personalities so they would not come up with unpleasant character surprises, and as much as she tried to set them with her words – 'always like that, so clumsy', 'always so reckless', 'always telling the same story' – people would always shift and change.

So the friends of her childhood were the only ones that had aligned themselves completely with my mother's visions. Even when their lives branched out in strange permutations and bore stranger fruit, she would try to find a way to link their narratives to the fixed seedlings in her head. Her childhood best friend, Ai Hua, was working at a Chinese restaurant because she had always been placid and family-orientated. Ai Hua was in her early fifties, and now an illegal immigrant in the United States, living in her boss's back room between the laundry and the toilet. She'd made it out of Vietnam in her mid-forties and had been living this illegal limbo life for seven years. During this time she had written letters to my mother. One of the letters attached a photograph of a smiling woman with her hair parted in the middle like the open pages of a book. She was standing in front of roses in a public park, far removed from what I imagined to be her usual sink space in a cramped back-corner kitchen.

'Don't go and visit her at her place,' my mother warned me when I was about to travel to America for a writing residency, 'because if the police catch her, you don't want to be involved.' My mother told me that I could meet Ai Hua in a public place, or ask her to visit me. Of course, my mother didn't know about the geography of a country with fifty states – Iowa was nowhere near New York City. My mother gave me a sheet of paper with a phone number on it. 'Give her a call,' she directed me, 'because I haven't heard from her for about two years. The last time she called she said that her mother had taken a fall in Vietnam. She told me that when she heard this, she cried all night until the morning.'

So I ventured off to the American Midwest, and I kept the phone number in the zipper pocket of my backpack, along with my passport. The first month was all about settling in, about eating as many foods made of corn starch and corn syrup and corn enzymes as I could, marvelling over the endless monotony of corn and soybean fields, and making friends with the other writers. I had deliberately delayed taking out the phone number and giving Ai Hua a call, out of a growing sense of unease that if I did it this early on in my residency, I would keep the woman waiting and waiting and hoping for my visit.

But a month later, I felt it was time, so I called the number in New York City.

'Allo?' It was a Chinese accent that answered.

'Could I please ask whether Auntie Ai Hua is there?' I asked in my inept Teochew.

'Who are you looking for?' a man demanded in Mandarin.

'Auntie Ai Hua,' I replied in infirm Mandarin.

'Who?'

I repeated the name. I was sure there was a slight pause of comprehension – even recognition – before the answer.

'Sorry, there is no one named that here.'

'Oh.' I paused. Should I ask again? No. He had made it clear that even if there was someone named that there, he was not going to tell me. 'Sorry. Thank you,' I muttered before I hung up.

'A man answered,' I told my mother the next time I called home. 'He spoke Mandarin, but he didn't know her.'

'It could be that her employer doesn't want her to have friends,' my mother replied matter-of-factly. Their men were their key to the outside world, but this key sometimes locked them housebound in strange foreign countries during the daylight hours.

'I could try again next week,' I suggested disingenuously, because we both knew that no matter how many times I called, I wouldn't find my mother's childhood friend on that number.

'Don't worry. It wasn't important anyhow,' my mother sighed. 'It's just as well. She might ask for money. And once they start asking, they will never stop.'

To my parents, 'friend' was not a Facebook verb. To *be* a friend attached an endless multitude of verbs – to love, to care, to provide, *to help in time of need.* So you either gave them your everything, or you didn't. Every true friendship they had had been tested through the treacheries of war and dragged through the killing fields, so that what remained was the heart of all that mattered. And what had remained was often not very much. So you had to be careful on whom you chose to spend this quota of affection. And like every migrant, my mother had chosen to spend it on her family.

Some people say I look exactly like my mother when I was her age. I don't really know because there are barely any photographs of her, and when she had children in her early twenties she set her hair permanently into a premature middle-aged perm. My mother never did hear from her best friend again, but perhaps she had been secretly hoping Ai Hua would be found, and that I, her daughter, would find her. Perhaps she yearned for this unlined image of herself to walk into the restaurant, a version that had not gone through war or displacement; and maybe she wanted to imagine the bafflement, the surprise, the ineffable and indelible joy on her friend's face: 'Kien! You haven't changed at all. Since we last saw each other in Vietnam, you really haven't changed at all!'

THE FIELD MARKER

EXECUTING HISTORY

T.S. Eliot wrote, 'I will show you fear in a handful of dust.' If you were to pick up a handful of dust, knowing that there was a high possibility that you were holding on to the literal remains of half your family, the half you will never meet – all the cousins and aunts and uncles and the grandfather that would have peopled your world but for the blunt-force trauma of the Pol Pot regime – what does that mean? And if your father, standing there right next to you, tells you that this is where he carried and buried them a few years before your birth, when the floods came, when they starved to death, when they closed their eyes with nothing but the scraps of black-dyed pyjamas covering their backs minus the buttons, would you bend to touch this earth? And how do you react when your father tells you quietly and matter-of-factly, 'The next year we planted crops in the same field. The rice grew twice as much, and twice as high.' What does it mean to write about fall and recovery? How do we look at history and make it matter when the past is dead, and to start all over again sometimes means to leave it buried?

These were the questions that preoccupied my mind for the past year, stemming from the trip I took with my father to Cambodia for the first time. A year later, I was standing in a different burial ground, still thinking about the same questions, but at the site of a different civil war that happened 150 years ago. Gettysburg is a town gently yet persistently preserved in its history. The pre–Civil War university, Gettysburg College (formerly known as Pennsylvania College), still stands today. The same building that was used as a war hospital on campus looks almost as it did 150 years ago on the outside. The battlefields are all still there, left flat and verdant as they were during the battle. The copse of trees from which the Confederates aimed at the Union base is still planted in the exact same position. The wooden fences have been recreated to look as they did one and a half centuries ago. Everything is still, because it's not tourist season yet; and everything is quiet.

This had been one of the bloodiest battle sites of the Civil War, a war in which more American soldiers were killed in the course of battle than in the Vietnam and Iraq wars combined. A loss on the same scale today, according to the sources at the Civil War Museum, would equal six million casualties.

Gettysburg had been a rural farming town of 2200, and only one civilian was reported to have been killed during the battle – a woman named Jennie Wade, who was baking bread in her house when she was hit by a stray bullet that went through two doors. The house in which she died is now a museum. It is incredible in this day and age to think that in a battle of 51,000 military casualties, only one civilian was killed.

But this war was not a civil one, fought brother between brother, as had been romanticised in the past for the purposes of achieving social cohesion in the new Union. This was clear when I saw photographs of piles and piles of amputated limbs, or pictures of all the bodies buried in shallow graves. As Professor Peter Carmichael of Gettysburg College led us through the battlefields, we stood in spots where thousands of men were killed in twenty minutes of battle, which later became the same place that the KKK held its rallies in the 1920s.

Today, confederate flags hang from shopfronts, and inside the souvenir stores you can buy grey (confederate) and blue (union) caps, Abraham Lincoln bobbleheads, and whole toy soldier packets for little children to re-enact the Civil War. I have to remind myself that this war was fought before the invention of plastic.

Almost every gift shop along Steinwehr Street advertises 'Real Civil War Relics', which largely consist of buttons and bullets. Everything back then, in the mid-nineteenth century, seemed organic except for bullets and buttons, everything melted back into the ground. But bullets and buttons – these were the only relics that did not decompose. Here, you can buy a bullet for three dollars (or four dollars for an unexploded bullet). I held a bullet in my hand. Encrusted with the lime of age, it was white and heavy, with a wide round tip. How strange to think that something so metallic, so inorganic, so tiny, could lodge in the living, breathing mass of a person. These Civil War soldiers back then would not have looked up at the sky to imagine that a little over fifty years later, tonnes of metal would be able to float in the atmosphere, able to drop iron eggs that exploded on the ground. Human beings can bring inanimate objects to life, but they cannot bring living creatures back from death.

So we preserve all that we can – the names of the regiments, the nameless remains at Arlington National Cemetery, the Gettysburg battleground, the letters from dead soldiers. In 1862, a college-educated northern lieutenant named Rush P. Cady wrote about sacrificing lives upon the altar of one's country:

The march of progress always goes through the battlefield. Good men have always fought to maintain & defend great principles. Good governments cost blood & treasure in the founding & also the preservation. The individual man is but a tool for the promotion of the progress & welfare of the whole race.

However, John Futch, a 26-year-old illiterate Southern soldier who dictated his letters home, felt differently. He was a New Hanover County man who owned three slaves. In his letter dated 19 July 1863, to his wife, he had just witnessed his brother's death:

Charley got kild and he suffered graideal from his wound he lived a night and a day after he was wounded we sead hard times thare … I am all … sick all the time and half crazy I never wanted to come home so bad in my life but it is so that I cant come at this time I want to come home so bad that I am home sick I want you to keep charleys pistol and if I ever git it back I will keep it … I staid with Charley until he died he never spoke after he was woundid until he died I never was hurt so in my life.

John Futch's letters home reveal an increasing desperation, homesickness, and escalating desire to be away from battle. His wife Martha's yearning for him sprawls across the pages ('dear husband I shal come to see you if you aint back by april for I want to see you veary bad'); but he wrote to tell her not to come to find him, reassuring her that he would be home soon. Shortly after the death of his brother Charley, Futch deserted the army. He was caught, sent back and executed in front of his fellow soldiers. The Confederate government made an example of John Futch's death: 'We do hope that the melancholy fate of these deluded men will … put a stop to the crime of desertion from the army.'

This was an era where post-traumatic stress didn't exist. Lieutenant Cady had left Hamilton College to fight in the war. While rallying his men on the first day of Gettysburg, he was struck by a minié ball and died of his injuries three weeks later. He was only twenty-two. Historians have asked whether his faith in heroic abstractions would also have survived if he too had survived the war. This was a time when personal feelings were subjugated for a greater cause, and the cause was meant to direct the course of a person's feelings. So what exactly was this greater cause? The survival of the Union, the fate of slavery, and the common rights of citizenship. Only two of these issues are resolved in the United States today.

Although there perhaps still exist some in the Southern states today who maintain that the Civil War was about the Southern states opposing the control of the new federal government, these states were largely agrarian economies dependent on slaves for the cotton trade. So this war was also undeniably about the right of Southern landowners to own slaves, which had been outlawed in the North in the very early part of the nineteenth century.

In the South, fewer than four slaves out of a hundred lived past the age of sixty. By the age of twelve, when a slave was sent to the fields, they had rotten teeth, worms, dysentery. Slaves, with their owners' consent, were allowed to marry, but their marriages were not recognised under law because they were considered chattels, not people. Preachers had to modify the wedding vows for them to till death or distance do us part, because slaves had three to four masters in their lifetimes. In 1860, four million men, women and children were slaves.

I went into Gettysburg Museum and saw the duplicate slave auction posters, which listed the slaves' ages, descriptions and prices. Some who were of 'unsound mind' or 'infirm' cost around

$200, others who were in their prime – and especially if they were of a 'high yellow' colour – were valued at over a thousand dollars. Beneath the poster would be a line stating: 'Some cattle, and farm-stock also available at auction' and 'As prices are so low, cash only'.

Even after the Civil War and the abolition of slavery, human beings were still regarded as chattels. When we visited Birmingham, we were guided around the town by Pamela King, a professor at the University of Alabama who teaches a subject called 'Mansions, Mines and Jim Crow'. Founded in 1871, Birmingham was a post–Civil War city, built during the middle of the Reconstruction era. Between 1875 and 1928, Alabama profited from a form of prison labour known as the convict-lease system. Under this system, companies and individuals paid fees to state and county govern-ments in exchange for the labour of prisoners. Professor King explained that when the city passed its first vagrancy act, anyone not working the very moment he was spotted by police could be arrested and taken to the county jails, and then transported to the Birmingham mines. Between 20 and 43 per cent of the miners died every year. Unlike slaves, who had a value because they were personal property, these convicts were entirely expendable. More than 95 per cent of county prisoners and 90 per cent of state pris-oners were African American, and whipping was the accepted norm for punishment.

From 1975 to 1979, Pol Pot of Cambodia and his Khmer Rouge soldiers also kept slaves, and they too did not buy or sell them. They all belonged to the revolution. The entire nation was divided up into different work collectives. Each collective consisted of a couple of thousand people, and they were worked to death or exe-cuted in the fields. That is why that area and era is known now as the killing fields. My father, along with the entire population of Cambodia, was kept working in Democratic Kampuchea, as the

I had not heard of the term 'American exceptionalism' until I was in the States. Somehow, to cultivate the idea that a group of people can be the chosen ones, can be gifted with a mission, can be blessed with an abundance that other countries in the world do not have, is to deliberately cultivate in the national psyche a guppie memory. But this selective spring clean-out of the country's history has been so successful that it is difficult to imagine overseas that America – a country which presents itself to the rest of the world as a unified force imbued with immeasurable wealth, modernity and power – was once a group of warring states divided by an ideology deep enough to rival that of North and South Vietnam in the 1960s. Of course, during the Vietnam War, the Civil Rights Movement was also taking shape in America. The Republican Party used to be 'the Party of Lincoln' while the Democrats in the South had imposed racial segregation by law. Steadily and stealthily, the course of history crept on and allegiances that men had once believed were immutable, allegiances for which they had even died, were now reversing, cooling, shifting. So to believe in any form of exceptionalism is to follow a narrative along a straight trajectory, like a bullet.

Yet to live in America is to know that there are places that have it much worse. Perhaps that is why some poor people in Morgan City, Louisiana and Alabama still have American flags planted firmly in the front yards of their properties, which house trailers or kit homes. Growing up in Melbourne, we lived in similar suburbs, but no one ever planted an Australian flag in the front yard.

When they first arrived in Australia and before their blind pursuit of the Australian Dream, our parents had friends. Most of them survived the killing fields; some fought in the Vietnam War; some were conscripted, like one of my uncles, who was pulled out of his village, an AK-47 shoved in his hands. Life in a democracy was baffling. The women sighed a lot; the men were reticent.

They were all scared of authority – the government, police, ticket inspectors on public transport, even parking inspectors. Sometimes they talked about the Black Thieves, which was what they called the Khmer Rouge. Yet with the glassy-eyed unfaltering optimism of a Gatsby, my father believed in the Great Australian Dream, which was very similar to the Great American Dream and all those 'Great Dreams' of democratic Western countries, lands of the free and homes of the brave: the unfaltering faith that if you worked hard enough and never gave up, success was inevitable. This belief was their buffer against trauma and being stuck in the quagmire of the past.

Barbara Ehrenreich writes in *The Dark Roots of American Optimism* about how the Calvinism brought to New England by the white settlers seemed to be a 'system of socially imposed depression', and how the movement towards positive thinking was a rebellion against the emotional austerity imposed by the Church and society. If you replace the religious purpose with political motivation, the following description sounds eerily like the ideology of a socialist dictatorship:

> The task for the Living was to constantly examine 'the loathsome abominations that lie in his bosom,' seeking to uproot the sinful thoughts that are a sure sign of damnation. Calvinism offered only one form of relief from this anxious work of self-examination, and that was another form of labor – clearing, planting, stitching, building up farms and businesses. Anything other than labor of either the industrious or spiritual sort – idleness or pleasure – was a contemptible sin.

Ehrenreich argues that the contemporary glo-white-smile brand of American optimism derived not from conformity but from a need to rebel against the Puritanical past. Instead of toiling to uproot evil from one's soul, one could work to enjoy the fruits of God's blessings. This was epitomised by the cheery and stoic wagon-progress mentality of the March sisters in *Little Women*, and as the decades progressed it gave rise to writers like Emerson, and later Norman Vincent Peale with his bestselling *The Power of Positive Thinking*. Yet when the complexities and problems with American identity and citizenship culminated in civil unrest, particularly in the '60s and '70s, people's peripheral vision could no longer be deliberately willed away. However, it could be distracted, with the ever-increasing lures of modern consumer society: things to own, things to be, things to eat.

The food in America looks and tastes good, in the way a child's drawing of food might be good: yellow corn. Orange cheese. Red ketchup. Bright violet yoghurt. No green except diluted in lettuce leaves. What is the rationale for inventing food that contains less nutritional value than eating a leather belt? Perhaps the logic is that poor people are only going to get hungry again anyway, so let's just focus on the taste of the food. Give the indigent a little bit of happiness before they lose their teeth and die of heart attacks inside their kit homes.

Travelling through Louisiana, we stayed in the Bayou Breaux Bridge Bed and Breakfast. I spent two nights in the 1950s Elvis cabin, a cheery little space decked out entirely in the vintage optimism of the era – plastic flowers; crocheted bedspread; black and white Laminex tiles; and, of course, the King all over the mirrors, hanging from the wall with one finger pointed towards the firmament, and even as an enormous plaster bust on top of a cupboard. But we ate well. We went to the Crazy '70s Bout Crawfish Cajun Café and feasted on boiled crabs, deep-fried Oreos and deep-fried bread and butter pudding.

We went to New Orleans, the Big Easy, where the food was slow and the music was fast. We watched the filming of the TV series *Treme*, met the creator David Simon, drank hurricanes and ate gumbo. Suddenly, this trip was beginning to become fun for me. It was beginning to remind me of my first trip to the States two years ago. Surrounded by its green paddocks and rows of cornfields, the University of Iowa was the ideal place for me to begin writing my first young-adult book. Two years later, I completed a book about a man who survived a genocide in Cambodia and his relationship with his daughter. The story that emerged had not been the story I had set out to write at all. After handing in the final edits, I set off for my second trip to the United States, on this Fall and Recovery tour, feeling much trepidation and anxiety about whether I should have written what I had.

Then I met Madeleine Thien, the extraordinary Canadian writer whose recent book, *Dogs on the Perimeter*, deals with memory and grief and reads like a gentle, heart-starting poem. Maddie and I spoke a lot about Cambodia. She had visited the killing fields and the genocide museum a number of times, and I learnt a lot from her about quiet courage. I also met Khet Mar, a Burmese writer who is on political asylum in Pittsburgh, and whose unfaltering knife-sharp sense of justice made me see the places we visited through new eyes.

We visited Greg Guirard, a Cajun fisherman, poet, writer and photographer who has lived his whole life in the Atchafalaya Basin. 'For a standard American,' Greg told us, 'if you're not making money, you're wasting time. For a real Cajun, if you're not having fun, you're wasting your life.' His homeland in the Atchafalaya Basin had been logged to death, all the ancient cypress trees rooted out of existence a generation before his birth.

The Atchafalaya Basin is very different from the rest of the

United States. The Cajun people seem to be from a different era and place, when time moved more slowly and stoicism was a virtue. In 1604, their ancestors left France for Acadia, now known as Eastern Canada. After the British conquest of Acadia, they were deported in 1755, and first arrived in Louisiana a year later. Roy Blanchard, Greg's friend, told us that 'a Cajun is a guy that's going to make it no matter what'. Greg writes that, 'We Cajuns are being Americanized, and some of us don't like it at all. The Cajun Dream and the American Dream are not the same.'

Greg and Roy took us out on a boat to the swamps of the Bayou. Greg's boat hauled up a catfish from a net. The catfish was enormous. At the bottom of the boat its gills opened and closed like someone flicking through the pages of a waterlogged book.

Roy invited us to his house and showed us a turtle that he had caught, a beautiful slow creature that he was going to eat. These men had lived their whole lives out here, and their happiness seemed to derive from a hard-won acceptance of the vicissitudes of life as subsistence fishermen and hunters, yet a way of life that is in danger of being eroded, like the land of the Atchafalaya Basin.

Most people have this deep-seated idea that a home is a place of warm comfort and simple safety, and so the notion of losing a home seems like losing all we have built in life, but it is more than that. Your home is a place where your suffering can take shelter. Homeless people in the street disturb us so because their misery is naked. There is nothing between them and the world, and the layers of grime and dirt and mental disquiet is often a result of being exposed alone in your suffering, whimpering in a place crowded with hurrying inhumanity. We hurry by because we are afraid, afraid there is nothing between us and them but very flimsy walls, nothing at all between the slave and the master but a layer of correctly coloured epidermis, nothing between the right side of the war and the wrong side except whose trigger finger works faster under pressure, nothing between the living and the dead but for the next breath.

Unless, of course, you have faith. Perhaps the Church is a place where one's suffering can truly find sanctuary. We visited two churches in the South. The first was an Evangelical church, with no altar and no cross. Instead, this sleek new place of worship consisted of just a modern hall equipped with all sorts of audio-visual equipment, and a rock band on stage. It was more a cross between a concert and a Tony Robbins seminar than a religious sacrament, and the pastor drilled into his predominantly white audience the lesson that they were God's Chosen People. They were there to make a difference – raising money for hurricane victims and evangelising. 'You are the aroma of Christ, so spread that aroma far and wide!' bellowed the pastor. Then they sang a hymn: 'God is Good, All the Time'.

The women of the church told us how they selected New Orleans flood victims to shelter: only families were chosen, and these families had to undergo background and criminal checks from the sheriff's department. They were given nine months to pull themselves together. These were people who had never before left their homes in New Orleans or set foot on a plane. Nine months to find jobs and restart their lives, or go back home. 'It is sad,' one lady of the church remarked to us. 'Some of them couldn't do it. They just fell apart.'

Of course, this is also what happens to 'Chosen People' when disaster strikes – it is an enormous and sometimes unbearable blow to one's self-belief. John Biguenet told us about the New Orleans doctors who took scalpels home while their surgeries were filling with floodwater; and how by the end of the weekend, they were dead. 'Imagine this,' John told us. 'You're fifty-five years old.

Your life has followed a certain successful and predictable path so far. You felt powerful and smart. But you have a mortgage on over a million dollars worth of surgical equipment in your clinic which you now can't repay because there are no more patients in New Orleans. You have a mortgage on a middle-class house. You have lost everything.' Imagine being bogged down by your attachments. I have heard stories of wealthy families who piled themselves and their children into their Mercedes-Benz when the city of Phnom Penh was being emptied of people. They drove their cars into creeks and rivers, choosing to die rather than confront the possibility of subjugation and hardship. Yet the Buddha said simply and unequivocally, life is suffering.

But take a look at us. We think we can control everything – our natural environment, other people, even our own bodies – and then when things seem beyond our control, when hurricanes hit, when levees break, when people die of dehydration on their rooftops, when we see masses of starving, huddled people, we recoil with horror. We don't think this sort of thing should happen. We insulate ourselves against the elements. Brad Pitt comes and builds a couple of beautiful, state-of-the-art, architecturally designed houses in New Orleans (even one shaped like a boat that will float away when the next flood comes), and that is the climax of the three-hour tourist 'Hurricane Katrina Bus Tour'. Ta-da! Recovery! We look through the bus windows, protected by a veneer of glass and moving vehicle, knowing that we are tourists who will go back to comfortable hotels, knowing we are writers who will go home to think about this long and deep and muster up the appropriate feelings of sympathy, moral outrage and guilt.

'After all that's happened to them, they smile so much.' People offer such polite charges of bravery to the people of Birmingham, Alabama; the people of New Orleans; the people of Burma; the people of Cambodia. We visit developing counties and remark about how happy the locals all look and how greedy we are back home, we toss the local children a few hundred riels and vow to change our own lives. Then we return to our quiet cul-de-sacs and forget. Maybe it is easier to take action to assuage our immediate feelings of guilt and feel good than it is to remember and reflect.

The second church we visited was the Sixteenth Street Baptist Church. This was the first all-black Baptist church of Birmingham, where many meetings during the Civil Rights Movement were held. Martin Luther King, Jr, visited this church, and so did the Ku Klux Klan. On 15 September 1963, they planted explosives in the basement that killed four black girls – Addie Mae Collins, Cynthia Wesley, Carole Robertson and Denise McNair – and injured more than twenty others. Twenty-six children at that time were walking into the basement assembly room to prepare for the sermon entitled 'The Love That Forgives' when that bomb exploded, and what was left of the face of Christ on the stained-glass window was a shattered hole.

Susan Sontag writes in *Regarding the Pain of Others*:

Someone who is permanently surprised that depravity exists, who continues to feel disillusioned (even incredulous) when confronted with evidence of what humans are capable of inflicting in the way of gruesome, hands-on cruelties upon other humans, has not reached moral or psychological adulthood. No one after a certain age has the right to this degree of innocence, of superficiality, to this degree of ignorance or amnesia.

Jesus said blessed are the meek for they shall inherit the earth, while poor Job sits there scraping his terrible skin with broken pieces of pottery. Perhaps both can coexist without the need to find evil in

Job or excoriate the meek. Without immediately rushing to make sense of suffering. This brings to the forefront a more fundamental question: is there a need to make sense of suffering at all?

What if all my genocide-surviving father wants to do with his new life is to start an electronics store in Melbourne, because in Democratic Kampuchea all forms of technology had been wiped out except the landmine, the AK-47 and the electric fence around Tuol Sleng? What if all my dad desires is to invest in a string of properties and confine himself to a leafy suburb, happily believing that the worst thing that could happen to me as a writer is a papercut? What obligation then do I have, as a writer, when I go back to dig up the past?

Last year when I visited Cambodia with my father, he was also going to go with me to Tuol Sleng, the death and torture prison that used to be an old primary school. In Tuol Sleng, faces stare at you from the walls, photographs of prisoners before execution. Not just men, but women with babies, children. Some of the faces have bloody noses, others have eyeballs beaten out of sockets; all are still alive but know they are going to die.

We never went in, never even came close to seeing the prison. Halfway there and entirely unrelated to our visit, I vomited in my uncle's car. I was just dehydrated, unaccustomed to the climate. The chauffeur drove us straight back to the air-conditioned comfort of my uncle's house, where my auntie sighed and said, 'See, you shouldn't visit such evil places. The bad spirits have gotten to you.' They took me instead to the Royal Palace, with its floor of silver tiles; to Angkor Wat, with its apsaras flying all over the columns; and to their private beach at Sihanouk Hotel. My family wanted me to see recovery, not annihilation. Yet how do I know about what is in Tuol Sleng prison? How can I describe the photographs, the bloodstains on the floor, the hairs stuck to the iron railings of the torture beds? These images are readily available to anyone – even a seven-year-old – if you enter in the right google terms. What makes the eyeballs of writers more legitimate? What makes historical suffering more 'real' than historical 'joy'?

And what does it mean to write about all this? Words are impermanent. Even books, which are physical objects, will get stuck in floods and become, as the playwright John Biguent said, 'the heaviest objects imaginable'. Professor Kent Gramm remarked to us during our meeting in Gettysburg, 'There is the belief that history is nothing except language piling on top of language.' What makes our transient thoughts real? If we stop thinking about trauma, does it exist? My cousins in Cambodia who survived Pol Pot can't remember a single thing about their childhoods during that era. Maybe the human body has a way of blocking off pain.

Blunt trauma needs to be alleviated by good health; love; success; and, dare I say, happiness. In America, in Louisiana, in Alabama, in Baltimore, in the Atchafalaya Basin, we did not see fulfilment of the American Dream. Sometimes we did not even see recovery. We met people like Greg Guirard who lamented the loss of their culture, Charlie Duff from Baltimore who mourned the disappearance of his stately city, and John Biguenet, who reminded us that 'the people of New Orleans have lived shoulder to shoulder with death since the founding of the city'. We listened to people like Mr Thomas Richard German, the 76-year-old gentleman who led us through the Sixteenth Street Baptist Church where the four black girls were killed. Mr German spoke about the changes he had seen in his lifetime and in his parents'. He told us how his father had worked for a white man and his children: 'When that lil' boy or girl turned eight, my father had to call them by their title, Master Alexander or Miss Emily.' He told us about how during the 1950s, sheriffs would pick up black men from the streets and castrate and kill them. How during the Civil Rights Movement, children were being arrested hundreds at a time and how the children actually enjoyed being taken in the police vans to the fairground to be processed. And how today, the most segregated day of the week in the United States is Sunday, when different groups go to their respective churches to hear about what makes a virtuous life, how to deal with loss and how to make sense of uncertainty.

We must not forget that the United States of America was built through an era of uncertainty. Perhaps the man who came closest to understanding this uncertainty was Abraham Lincoln. It is unlikely that a man like that would ever be elected in today's current political environment. Lincoln lacked the charisma that is so necessary for television politics today, but more significantly he suffered from severe bouts of depression. 'A tendency to melancholy,' Lincoln wrote, 'let it be observed, is a misfortune, not a fault.' Yet that this mournful leader should deliver words that would rouse a nation at war defies all modern perceptions that depressed people are lackadaisical, are passive and should be heavily medicated. It also makes me wonder whether American culture now puts too much emphasis on the emotions, as if they were the sole barometer of one's existence. In order to be a respected independent and adult human being, we are taught to be affirmative and preface our sentences with 'I feel', 'I think', 'I know'. What if there was just feeling, thought and knowledge that did not belong to 'me' or 'I'? Then perhaps we would be more forgiving of self-doubt, sadness, reticence. We would not have to talk all the time to justify ourselves. And perhaps then, melancholia would not be a personal fault but a misfortune.

In his 1863 Gettysburg address, Lincoln said: 'The brave men, living and dead, who struggled here, have consecrated it, far above our poor power to add or detract.' This address, less than three hundred words long, endured throughout history as one of the most powerful speeches of all time. These words move because Lincoln does not try to 'own' these men or their deaths. Lincoln does not cloak their cadavers in posthumous finery.

Standing on the battlefields of Gettysburg was an emotional experience for me. For a year, I couldn't write about the field in Cambodia and its dust of people without feeling like I was making them up, because I did not know them. All the buried cousins and all the starved uncles, all the small babies. All those meaningless deaths leaving behind nothing. I think perhaps this is what Lincoln means by our 'poor power to add or detract'. Lincoln understood what it was like to rise above emotion without superimposing optimism. Involuntarily blinkered by depression all his life, Abraham Lincoln never voluntarily willed away his peripheral vision.

I felt very lucky to take part in this tour. What amazed me most was that the US Department of State would take a group of writers from around the world to show them not the best parts of the country – the thriving industries, the lively culture and art, and the booming cities – but the side of the country in the shadows. Perhaps no other country in the world would open itself up so liberally to literary ambassadors from other nations. Through the University of Iowa's Writers in Motion program, freedom of speech in America is real, and it thrives.

On my flight returning to Australia, my thoughts about my two-week journey were interrupted by my neighbour. I was seated next to a middle-aged gentleman who had teeth as white as a picket fence. He was everything an accomplished American man should be. Son of strict Eastern-European immigrants, he defied his parents' expectations and married a girl with hair the colour of cornfields. At one point in his life, he was sleeping in his car because his father had kicked him out of home. So he started his own business. Both his sons became professional sportsmen, which was why he was heading down to Australia, to see one of them perform in a world championship. He told me that anything was possible if you only worked hard enough for it, and believed in it enough, and were a decent person. He asked me what I had been doing in the States for two weeks, and I told him that I had been looking at disaster and resilience. A few hours before our plane landed, he asked me extensive questions on how he would go about writing his life story. But I had a creeping suspicion that he already knew how.

We had started our journey on a battleground in Gettysburg, and ended it in a burial ground at Arlington General Cemetery in Washington, where the past was set in stone monuments, to be travelled across through well-paved pathways. Between these hushed places, we visited cities and heard the voices of people in these cities. We saw the parts of America where people were trying to eke out a life, trying their best to retain their separate cultures, people mourning loss, people being honest and resilient in quiet and unassuming ways. People forgotten by the narrative of quick success that is pivotal to the popular culture of the States today. The melancholy president, the common soldier, the Cajun fisherman, the middle-class church mother, the son of the Civil Rights Movement and the optimistic father – all these people formed part of a common history. Before we left New Orleans, John Biguenet told us that 'art is not about opinion. It is about human beings living.'

THE FIELD MARKER

Our father would never let me travel to South-East Asia when I was a student, so the first time I visited Cambodia was when I was twenty-nine, with him and my sister Alison. In the plane, he warned us about the smallness of the airport, the dirtiness of the streets and the poverty of the people. He described the landmines and the lepers. It was as if he had raised us the way Siddhartha was raised – safely ensconced from all the possible perils of the world – so that the first time we saw sickness, ageing and death, we would feel like our insides were sucked dry. He wanted us to be prepared.

Our father was twenty-three when Pol Pot's army marched into Phnom Penh, on 17 April 1975. They were an army of children. Their skin was brown. Their hair shone orange. Their eyes were oysters in two moons. They looked around, moving slowly, as if they were lost. Theirs was the breath of small animals in the night. It was as if they had not been taught how to walk, eat or laugh, but had learnt these things by doing them. Every sense woke up when they reached the city. Many of these boys had never been inside a city before, so every stimulus could only be predatory. Their uniforms were pyjamas dyed black as night, and some carried their AK-47s upright, as though they were going to set off fireworks.

They were children who had never tasted candy, to know that this was the stuff you were meant to steal from the shops. Instead, they smashed things up. Children with guns, children with bang-bang-shoot-them-dead-I-kill-you-long-time-Mister minds. Kill was a long time; dead was even longer. This was the only truth they knew. When they looked up at the sky they did not see the fingers of God; they saw the direct cause of death of their parents, the American bombs.

The only modern marvels they had seen were the stick of a gun, the iron bird in the sky and the green disc on the ground. But what was a stick of gum? A block of paper fastened at one end? What was a globe of the world? A balloon? What was a cinema? A grandfather clock inside a house? If you didn't know anything, how did you know it was not a new sun that crawled up over the fields every day? How did you know that the earth was not flat? They didn't, but they were assigned the task of taking over the only world our father had ever known. And during their reign, they had assigned our father the task of burying the dead on higher ground when the floodwaters came.

During peacetime, the yearly floods would wash over the vegetation, leaving behind rich level soil. But during the reign of slavery the floods that came completely washed away the sweet potato leaves, wild weeds and grasses that the people had come to depend upon for food. People would just collapse in the fields and their bodies would be there days later, next to the workers, beside them, beneath them, as they worked. In the village next to our father's, the whole collective of more than three thousand people – except their four Khmer Rouge soldiers – had perished.

In his own collective, half-living people were assigned to carry off the dead to elevated ground and bury them. Our father was assigned the task with another man. With a blanket between the two of them, they would hoist the body out of the floodwaters and onto the blanket. He and his companion would then each take an end of the blanket and heave it onto their shoulder. A walking hammock. One last free ride for the dead. Except it wasn't a very stable ride. They were so malnourished and weak that they kept slipping and falling into the water. Each time they fell, the blanket would become more waterlogged and heavy.

'Don't worry,' our father's friend told him, 'just look forward to the day when others will be carrying you off wrapped up nicely in a blanket and getting more attention than the living ever did.'

'Maybe I'll be the one giving you the special treatment,' our father replied.

'What do you mean? Sweet Bodhisattva, I hope you're not going to be this heavy when it's my turn to heave you out of the floodwaters!'

A few weeks later, our father was assigned with another man. They were both silent on their first journey, carrying the blanket containing his nameless friend whom this new companion had replaced. They walked uphill, dug a shallow grave, placed the body in carefully, and then scooped a light mound of dirt over it.

*

Now, thirty-one years later, we were heading back to the field where our father had buried all the dead. We came in a convoy of SUVs and Mercedes-Benz, all owned by our Uncle Kheav. Uncle Kheav was our father's older brother. He had also survived the killing fields and was now an immensely successful bank CEO and property developer. Former soldiers who were now my uncle's personal bodyguards surrounded us wherever we went, because our uncle did not want any of us to be kidnapped for ransom. The cars stopped in front of an empty white field and we all got out: our father, sister, Uncle Kheav and our auntie.

My senses stretched, working their hardest to take in the world. At first there was the field. And the heat, when the sky breathed its fever breath over the field. Then back to the field and its unyielding dust. Nothing grew on it. Yet once death here had hot halitosis that withered away the bodies much faster, and the field was used to plant crops during each following season. 'The best fertiliser in the world,' our father told us. 'When I was digging up the ground to plant the next season of rice, I unearthed the small wooden marker of your auntie's mother's burial spot.'

'Did you stow it away and keep it?' I asked.

'No, of course not. If you even picked up a handful of dirt from the ground, you were stealing from the revolution.'

'People dug the graves up, over and over again, after the liberation,' Uncle Kheav told me. They were looking for rings and gems looped around finger bones and wrists.

'There was nothing,' our father said. 'When I buried those bodies, they didn't even have proper clothes.'

Now there were not even any bones left. None of those people seemed to have existed, and yet the SUV played a slow Cambodian dirge, and our auntie was kneeling on the floor in front of an incense urn she had placed on the soil, with three sticks of incense clutched in her hand. When she rose up after her third bow and turned around, her shoulders were shaking with the memory of her mother.

It hit me at last: Dad buried bodies here, I realised, bodies in each handful of dust. Bodies of strangers, and people he had worked with, known as family, and loved. Bodies that needed to be held, that needed to move and exhale and blink, just as we were doing. Bodies no one will ever remember, not like the skulls in stupas that Westerners always wanted to visit. By now our father was looking elsewhere, away from our auntie, who was weeping over her dead mother. He pointed to the trees. There weren't many, and they were skinny coconut or sugar palms huddled by the edges of the yellow field, as if afraid to step into the soil of a million souls.

'Look at those bamboo ladders attached to the trees,' he said. 'They're used for climbing to the very top, to collect coconuts or the juice of sugar palms.' I grabbed on to the ladder and started up.

'Only the first few rungs,' he said, 'or you could fall and die.'

I let go, and didn't bother to try.

I felt that the country was something precious – brutal, split open like a pomegranate, with a million hidden red and buried eyes. It was a visceral land, a land that gave me strange dreams at night: dreams of Job sitting in the middle of his burnt-out house, his children dead, scraping at his skin with bits of broken pottery, set in a prelapsarian paradise. It was a land of earth and water where the living people lived; and a land of wind and fire where the dead were cremated and malingered over hot fields.

I watched as my uncle's bodyguard carefully dug a hole in the ground and lit a fire in there, so that my auntie could burn heaven banknotes for her mother. My auntie wanted to make sure her mother, stripped of everything in life, had enough in the afterlife.

'You must remember your ancestors,' said the ex-soldier who was now my uncle's bodyguard, 'and honour them.'

THE BUS

It was when she was sick that she first realised her father would do anything for her. She must have been about five. She woke up in the middle of the night, and he made her jam on toast. Then, when she had heavy asthma at eleven and was housebound for two weeks, he bought her ice-cream, the expensive kind, with real strawberries in it. But when she was really little, about four, she had the flu and had some idea about death. She whimpered on the couch and said, 'Dad, I don't want to die.'

'Be quiet and drink this Milo,' he told her, rubbing Vicks Vaporub on her chest.

Her father, she noticed as she grew older, never used the words death or die, unlike her mum and grandmother and aunties. If they dropped something, it was 'Si oh!' *Go die.* If they made a mistake. If they heard some bad news, such as their child getting less than 90 per cent in an exam. But her father never uttered it.

There were some things they would never mention again, like the box-cutter boy. And other things that he didn't mind her finding out. 'If you want to know about the time of Pol Pot, I will introduce you to people,' her father told her a year after the box-cutting incident, 'and they will talk to you and tell you about their lives.'

He took her to visit his friends in suburban houses with neat front yards in Footscray and Springvale, and they would tell her tales of survival. She remembered these moments, how at some pivotal point these older folk began to speak to her as if they no longer saw her as a child but as someone who would store these stories, and who might one day convey them to their own progeny, who were too preoccupied with building houses and bringing up babies to sit and listen.

There they both were, she and her father, sitting on a couch in a strange man's house. The man, a friend of her father, was a furniture-maker. He had made the couch himself. She looked at him, and then looked back down at the couch. How could a man as thin as that make a thing of wood and leather as robust as the sofa set they were all sitting on? She realised her father and she sat in the exact same way. They perched on their tailbones at the very edge of the seat, as if to sink back and get comfortable would be to indulge themselves.

Perhaps this story was not meant to begin on a bus in China at all.

Perhaps it was meant to begin on another bus, in another place, during another time.

The bus, the man said. It loaded us on, and then took us to the top of a mountain and dumped us there. The mountain was dotted with landmines. At the top there was no food or water, so we went down and exploded and died.

But the man was sitting in front of them, telling this story, so obviously he had not died. Neither had his wife, who was serving them cups of tea. Chinese cups were very small, she realised. You could not hug them in your hands and lean back on a couch, ready for a yarn. The size of a cup was probably the measure of a society's loquaciousness. You couldn't tell a long-winded story about a visit to the supermarket while holding a Chinese cup with two fingers. Its contents were two gulps. The end. So your story needed significance, but not the kind of tall-poppy significance that would upstage your friend. One thing those who came from Cambodia were good at doing was keeping quiet and listening. Another thing was telling a story using the most direct route, like that bus carrying those people she would never meet. Depositing them like a dumpster at the precipice of a very high tip. Who was the first at the top of the mountain to start worrying, she wondered, and the first to make their way down?

She may never know what happened, but perhaps it was time for her to take a stab in the dark.

WRITING ABOUT MY FATHER

Anaïs Nin wrote, 'If you do not breathe through writing, if you do not cry out in writing, or sing in writing, then don't write, because our culture has no use for it.'

Writing my second book took a lot out of me. In 2008, I went to Beijing as part of an Asialink residency, to try and write about my cultural roots. Roots of a culture begin with the ground, and so I was hoping for an epiphany of sorts, hoping that when I reached my grandmother's Chinese ancestral town of Jie Yang, Chaozhou, that I would be able to see the earth as sacred and feel a connection. But when I arrived I saw that a modern developed city – complete with its own McDonald's – had grown out of the foreign country that my grandmother had described to me in my childhood. L.P. Hartley wrote that 'the past is a foreign country: they do things differently there'. It felt impossible to write about a place in which I had no immediate connection, and so I returned to Beijing. Even though I tried to write 'cultural' stories during my stay, they became amusing anecdotes with no substance, like a *qipao* without a body. One or two of the stories ended up being at the very beginning of *Her Father's Daughter*; my editors liked them even though I was embarrassed by them. In retrospect, they needed to be there to mark my development. They are there to show that progress requires letting go of this idea of perfection. Ironically, they are also the pieces I worked on the longest – I was polishing something that did not have much mettle.

The real heartbeat of the story emerged when I called my father up in the evenings from my small flat in Peking University. He wanted to know that I was warm and safe, and he also wanted to tell me about the bushfires that were raging through Victoria at that time. Even though we lived nowhere near Kinglake, and even though my father had never been there, he was deeply affected by the government allowing residents to 'stay and defend' their houses. 'How can property matter more than people?' he lamented. That evening when I got off the phone, I thought about my father preparing for bed, and how he would lock every door of the house and close every window. He would make sure all the knives were in their proper place in the drawers. And every knife would have had its tip deliberately filed to a blunt nub. This is when I realised that instead of trying to set my story in an 'exotic' location (which rendered all descriptions two-dimensional and florid), the tale was meant to take place in Melbourne, my place of birth and home. And I also realised that the story was going to be completely character-based, about my relationship with my father.

After working out that the story had to be from the perspective of a sixty-year-old man, I knew that a first-person narrator with my father's 'voice' would not work. First, because I am a 31-year-old female, it would be presumptuous to think that I could write in the voice of someone with sixty years of life experience. Second, because my father thinks in a different language than I do, I would have had to translate his thoughts, and I could find no way to do this that would not make him sound like he was speaking 'broken' or incomplete English in first person. I also discovered that the more I wrote in third person, the freer I felt as the narrator.

A first-person narrator is not going to be noticing how the streaks of sunset looked like a claw across the sky when they are ploughing the fields as a slave labourer with an AK-47–toting soldier standing next to them. All of a sudden the world of 1975 Cambodia emerged in its technicolour horror because I could use a wider lens.

Since my father's voice was in the third person, and this book is a 'conversation' between a father and a daughter, I could then not put myself, the 'daughter narrator', in the story in first person. To write about myself in first person while leaving my father in third is to try and own a significantly larger portion of the story than I was due: a reader would probably then read the book as me *telling a story about my father, from my perspective.* I wanted both voices to have equal weight and gravitas. Interestingly, Doris Lessing observed that it is actually the first-person narrator that alienates, because the capital 'I' is specific, whereas the third-person voice is general – the reader could be 'she'. I wanted the reader to feel like this could be *any daughter*, and *any father*, if trapped in the particular set of circumstances of this specific father–daughter relationship.

Many people have assumed that I wrote about the character of myself in the third person as a distancing technique, but this is not true. I saw much more of myself and my flaws in third person than I ever did in first. Unhindered by my voice in my first book, which was the voice of a twenty-something armed to the teeth with caustic wit and black humour, I learned to lay down these weapons and be more vulnerable to the reader. As a result, I have not read back over, or even looked at, the 'daughter' parts of the book since it has been published. To me it is almost like reading back on a private diary I thought I had shredded years ago.

Lastly, the most confronting chapters of the book, the chapters that have given writers like Alex Miller nightmares and disturbed reviewers no matter how kind the review, seem so jarring to a reader because I did not follow a conventional chronological structure. Year Zero in Democratic Kampuchea (17 April 1975, a date etched forever in my parents' memories) does not happen at the start of the book but two-thirds of the way in. In fact, this is the inverse migrant success story: it begins with the fulfilment of the Great Australian Dream, about a man who is so comfortable in life that he lives in a mansion on top of a hill in one of the safest suburbs in Melbourne and runs a thriving electronics business. His children can travel the world and he can Skype them. Yet everything he does is permeated by inordinate levels of anxiety.

This story is about a paring back to the bare bones of the narratives that shape a man's life. You find out that he lived for four years without modern technology, running water, medicine and, often, food. Yes, it is a story about privation, but the privation chapters could not come *first*. This is because no writing ever exists in isolation of the social and political context in which it was written. I do not set out to write 'refugee' stories, mainly because a refugee is 'one who seeks refuge' from both a Buddhist perspective and an international law perspective ('owing to a well-founded fear of being persecuted', Article 1, *United Nations Convention Relating to the Status of Refugees*). When a person stops fleeing and finds sanctuary, they are no longer a refugee.

Yet the 'refugee success' narrative works because it garners people's sympathy and affection, particularly when humour is used to enhance the poignancy of the narrative. I know how to tell this story – I have been doing it for over seven years in my talks to rural groups and inner-city book clubs and schools. When I do tell it I am entirely sincere, but I am also aware of my audience: I know that tacitly certain audiences do not want to hear tales of hardship. In fact, my father's concern and his only comment about the book, upon reading all the chapters I emailed him, was, 'Do you think there is too much suffering in this part? White people don't want to hear about too much suffering. It depresses them.'

Yet I had to take risks with this book. I wanted to counter the narrative that the only migrant or refugee story worth telling is one that leads to worldly 'success' and assimilation at the end. Chaim Potok wrote beautiful, intensely deep stories about the Hasidic Jewish community in the United States who were distinctly 'un-assimilated', yet his books opened our worlds to a richly developed and nuanced culture. It is deeply disappointing to me that we are a nation of immigrants and yet we need to keep our complex and multifaceted true selves *apart*, in order to be *a part* of this national narrative.

If I placed the more shocking 'killing fields' chapters of the book first, the book would inevitably and simply follow the migrant trajectory of 'success', but my father would always be seen as an eternal 'refugee' because our current mainstream discourse about 'those who've come across the seas' is polarising and unsophisticated. And I am well aware that no one will take literary non-fiction seriously in this political climate if it is about a contentious political issue. One of my favourite poets, Robert Cording, says this very useful passage about writing poetry, which I believe to be equally applicable to writing creative non-fiction:

> If the poem feels like it has sifted and arranged received ideas, then it will fail. The person has to feel, I think, as if there's a real person struggling with real experiences that will not yield some handy lesson, but nevertheless is not entirely without meaning. The voice that convinces will always be the voice of an individual, not as a spokesperson for this or that idea.

So this is not a story culminating in grand triumph over adversity – if anything, it is about very ordinary things beneath which lie the true character tales: a father who does not believe in post-traumatic stress yet files the tips of every knife in the house to a blunt nub, and a daughter who goes to an inner-city dating agency because her parents are setting her up before she is 'on the shelf' at twenty-five. I wanted to combine the everyday, Anne Tyler–type events of my father's current life in suburban Australia with the blinding flashes of unimaginable apocalyptic hell, to create a new kind of art that says quietly but clearly – this is how survivors live and love: slowly, patiently and doggedly.

To write a grandiose heroic tale about my dad would be true but annoying, as most people think their fathers are heroes: how could any of them compare to a man who survived genocide? Yet to write a book that is *more true*, I had to write about the parts of my dad in which a reader would find *every dad*. You don't need to survive trauma to fear for your kid's safety. You don't have to be cut off from modern civilisation to be in childlike awe over emerging new technologies. And you don't have to be a hero to be able to love wholeheartedly.

AT SCHOOL
AND ON THE PAGE

KATHARINE'S PLACE

I am in Greenmount, Western Australia. The sign outside the house says 'Katharine's Place', but I didn't realise that her husband was still here, until Mardi told me. When she told me, I was staring at a bird in the gutter, at how the colours of death made it look so alive. Its wing and tail feathers were spread out in blue and yellow Crayola tones. The feathers on its neck looked like the fur of a bonsai rabbit. Bright red organs puffed out from the middle of its chest, like an external heart too large for its body. This was no factory chicken that had never seen the light of day, no endless writhing of suffering hung upside down by its legs to meet its end in spinning blades. This was some tropical glory of creation, smashed by a vehicle in a car park in suburban Perth.

'Are you afraid of ghosts?' Mardi asked.

It depended on what kind of ghosts they were.

'Sometimes you can hear the footsteps of Hugo Throssel walking through the house.' He was Katharine Susannah Prichard's husband, and Mardi told me that when she stayed at Katharine's Place, she had heard his footsteps. 'But don't worry,' she said. 'He's a benign ghost.' Throssell was a celebrated war veteran: he fought in Gallipoli and won the Victoria Cross during World War I. He had taken his own life at this house during the Great Depression, while his wife was overseas promoting her books.

I am staying at Katharine's Place for a writer's residency. Mardi May, a local author and editor, picked me up from the airport and took me to the market so I could buy a week's supply of groceries, because I will be quite secluded in the house. I arrive to a house full of friendly helpers, the committee members who kept Katharine's Place alive, co-ordinated by Lynn Gumb, chair of the Katharine Susannah Prichard Writers' Centre. 'We're fixing your house for you,' Lynn tells me. Old wooden furniture is being moved back in after the floorboards have been shined, including the piano David Helfgott used to play when he visited. I help unpack a box of gifts that were given to Katharine: books, paintings, a boomerang and a wooden spear. Some of the things are very old, because she lived here for most of her life, from 1919 to 1969. Through three generations, my family has not even lived in one country for that long, and we do not own anything made before 1980.

This is the house in which Katharine Susannah Prichard, born in 1883 with 'ink in her veins', worked to become one of Australia's first internationally acclaimed authors. She wrote in her autobiography, *Child of the Hurricane,* that 'the happiest years of my life were spent in our home at Greenmount in the West. My best literary work was done there.' She had spent the first ten years of her married life in this home, and as newlyweds she and her husband used to disport themselves 'like Adam and Eve in the garden' overlooking the Perth hilltops.

Soon everyone leaves, and I am alone in the house to get on with my business. My parents would be alarmed if they knew about the nature of the place – 'Taking annual leave to spend it in a house with ghosts!' – so when I call home in the evening, I don't tell them about the noises. The first night, when I hear the creaks, I turn on the radio and sleep with it through to morning. But then

I hear footsteps during the day, too. I start to listen closely. Up and down the wooden floorboards. Small animals do not walk upside down beneath floorboards.

Sometimes there seems to be more than one person walking, probably because Katharine also died here, in her old age. The locals called her the Red Witch of Greenmount, and when there were government raids she used to hide her communist propaganda in the now-heritage-protected plumbago bushes outside the house. She had truly believed in communism:

> it was the answer to what I had been seeking: a satisfactory explanation of the wealth and power which control our lives – their origin, development, and how, in the processes of social evolution, they could be directed towards the well-being of a majority of the people, so that poverty, disease, prostitution, superstition and war would be eliminated; peoples of the world live in peace, and grow towards perfecting their existence on this earth.

My grandmother was a communist too, back in China. Her parents sent her to the Chaozhou teachers' college, where she learnt to read and write, and soon she decided to write about landlords abusing the rights of the peasants. Her writing sent her into exile, to Cambodia; she came to Australia when in her seventies. She taught me Buddhist sutras to chant in the dark. She knew the Heart Sutra off by heart and could even sound it out phonetically in Pali.

When my grandmother died, I hoped that she would walk our house, but she had never stayed a night in our new home. She was very sick before she died; she lay in bed for six years, blinking at the ceiling. Some things she saw there made her very sad, and on rare occasions some things made her laugh. After a while, I realised she wasn't seeing things in the ceiling, but in her mind.

There was a writer at Katharine's Place in the early '90s who needed to bring in an exorcist – but Grandmother wasn't scared of benign ghosts, so neither am I. Benign ghosts were white people, the ones who took such good care of my family when they came to Australia. My grandmother would have liked Katharine Susannah Prichard, a beautiful woman whose photographs grace the walls of the house, her face smiling beatifically at her first Asian author-in-residence. When Katharine was alive, society still considered people like me to be the Yellow Peril.

At the end of my residency, I ask Mardi again about the ghosts. 'Oh, who knows?' she says reassuringly. 'Sometimes the wind makes noises. And it's an old house. It creaks.' But I did hear footsteps, I tell Mardi. A quiet and steady amble, and sometimes small scuffling sounds. My grandmother also had a shuffling walk: her feet were afraid to be far from the ground, in case she fell over.

'I can't believe you were told about the ghosts on your first day,' Aminah, a songwriter and the caretaker of the writers' centre, says. 'You weren't meant to know that until the end of your trip.' But I am glad Mardi told me. Perhaps there is no ghost, but I would be disappointed if that were the case. We all see what we want in our heads.

SCHOOL DAYS

'Ladies' is such a salacious word when slurred by young men, but when enunciated by a carefully coiffured middle-aged lady to a mass of Year 10 girls it is a severe admonition not to move. I wondered how long it would take to set the limbs of adolescent restlessness.

'Settle down, young *lay-dees*.'

Less than a minute. Impressive.

I stood on the auditorium stage, being told off in front of 350 fifteen-year-olds in blue ties and heavy shoulder pads. This had never happened to me before, and it wasn't even my school.

The head of English wanted to make a speech before introducing me: 'Alice Pung has arrived ten minutes late, and she *apologises for coming late*, lay-dees.' I apologised and offered to make up the lost time. No longer feeling like a lawyer approaching thirty, or the visiting author the school had invited to inspire its students, I had the sensation that my stomach was dropping to the floor. I had forgotten schools could have this kind of effect.

During my adolescence, I changed high school five times. I traversed the whole Victorian education system: public state schools, private religious (Catholic) schools, private grammar schools and public selective state schools. And now, every year during Book Week, I talk to secondary students around the country.

Book Week was set up in 1945 as a time to spend celebrating Australian authors and illustrators. But some schools can afford to spend more than others, as I soon found out.

One ladies college invited me to speak at their school assembly for ten minutes, and told me proudly that I was their 120th guest speaker for the year. Two beautiful girls greeted me. With their blazer lapels so heavily impaled with merit pins – debating, swimming, drama – they looked like young lieutenants in the army, and like they had just stepped out of a Nordic Colours hair-dye commercial. They escorted me to the stage for assembly, where I peered down at hundreds of pretty, passive faces. Two words ballooned inside my head: polite boredom. The discipline it takes for these girls to sit still with their hands in their laps is extraordinary. I mustered all my energy, wishing to do justice to the inordinate fee I was being paid, but as I spoke I felt like the 120th courtesan in line.

When I'd finished speaking, I braced myself for another telling off. 'That was very interesting,' came the response from the head of English. It is easy to tell when a teacher has not really understood what I have been talking about. Even after I show slides of Cambodia in the time when my family fled from there – of the killing fields, dismembered bodies, bloodied faces – the same adjective pops up, like a twisting of that old Chinese adage: may you live in interesting times.

Afterwards, the principal invited me to a lunch of white-bread sandwiches cut into tiny triangles, with a small smear of salmon paste on them, or cucumber, or lettuce and tomato – vegetables low in calories because they are mostly water. The young ladies folded napkins neatly on their laps and picked out a triangle each. At the coaxing of their principal, some asked me about university and entrance scores. Most of these girls were headed for university in the next couple of years. Their futures stretched before them like a string of numbers, and I wondered how much they were allowed to focus on the immediate, to be allowed to concentrate on living in the moment, rather than seeing everything as a means to the end of adolescence. They reminded me of hot-house strawberries: lushly beautiful but easily bruised.

In every school there are teachers who are the most caring of people, but it is the collective culture of a school that is the first thing an outsider notices. It has a lot to do with how much natural laughter is allowed before students are deemed to be behaving in a manner ill becoming young ladies and gentlemen.

'Miss, can I give you a hug?' asked a skinny fourteen-year-old Asian girl before I left the Catholic college in Springvale, where I had told stories to the students for an hour. She reminded me of my little sister. In fact, the whole year level reminded me of my siblings, and I wanted to hug them all. The teacher gave an indulgent smile, and suddenly I was surrounded by en-masse embracing. Being treated nicely is not the same as being blessed with kindness, and there are some schools that are really, really kind – you feel it as soon as you walk in the door.

Most of my secondary schooling was spent in single-sex schools, but I had never visited an all-girls boarding house until I arrived at Walford, in Adelaide. I came at 10.30 in the evening, ready to spend the next day conducting writing workshops. Seona, the teacher on duty, took me upstairs to my bedroom. The boarding house was not a year old, and this room was meant for mothers staying over with their daughters: it was feminine, tidy and the colour of lollies. A sherbet-coloured bedspread covered each of the twin single beds, and in the bathroom were clean cocoa-brown towels. The place looked good enough to eat. I realised I had not yet had dinner, so one of the teachers brought me up a plate of roast pork and vegetables.

The next morning, the school librarian took me to the students.

'A real-life author!' Alison told Grade Six. I felt like a giant, with them seated on the floor while I stood and told my stories. The older girls, who were studying my book, did not ply me for answers to essay questions. Instead of polite attentiveness, there seemed to be genuine interest – in storytelling, writing, books. The day was suffused with laughter.

That evening I met the girl boarders: from rural Australia, Thailand, Hong Kong, South Korea. I was happy to see that they ate like healthy girls. I sat with them in the common room while Amara, from the Northern Territory, gave me a new hairstyle. Jenny, from Taiwan, showed me a photograph of her three-month-old brother. These girls – even the ones in Year 11 – still needed a pass to cross the road to the shops. But almost all were interested in the world outside their heads.

At one private boys school, I spoke at the Literature Club dinner. Like the girls in their sister school, a ladies college, these were well-behaved and highly intelligent students. But when they spoke, I got a strange jolt – I was hearing one thing and seeing another. The fourteen-year-old boys, many of whom were Asian and Indian, had the assurance, cadences and vocabulary of sophisticated middle-aged Englishmen (but, fortunately, not their teeth). Standing by the mantelpiece, awaiting their turn at the lectern, they seemed peculiarly colonial. They presented reports replete with phrases such as 'remarkable narrative', 'meandering plot', 'conscious effort to disconcert the reader'.

The boys with whom I grew up were mostly boys without words, boys capable of inordinate bouts of rage and tenderness, boys with the dangerous physical mix of itchy knuckles and firm deltoids. They were likely to beat the crap out of young men who used words such as 'remarkable'. Fortunately, in my experience, the two worlds rarely met. While one group was studying S.E. Hinton's tale of class divides and power struggles among rival gangs, the other was studying a story told in iambic pentameter of two rival gangs 'alike in dignity'.

During my high-school years, I was a participant in both of those groups, at schools on the opposite sides of the spectrum. In Year 8, at a girls Catholic college mostly filled with migrant children, we studied John Marsden's *So Much to Tell You*, about Marina, a deeply scarred girl who did not speak but wrote in her diary. Ms Clarke never used the words 'text' or 'analyse'. She got us to perform role-plays: 'You have to be *any character* other than Marina,' she advised. At home I wrote a script on tissues using a typewriter. I got up in front of the class as Marina's hysterical mother, spending ten minutes 'crying' into my notes. The class laughed, but in a good way. Ms Clarke had a rare knack for taking us outside ourselves, and of bringing out the painfully shy students.

At my grammar school, we studied John Keats' 'La Belle Dame Sans Merci'. Our literature teacher told us it was about the artistic muse using the poet and leaving him drained. Stephen said it was just about a guy's sexual obsession with a chick. 'Look at this, miss! She found him *roots* of relish sweet!'

'Aw, come on – if you can read sex into that, you can read it into every line,' said our teacher.

So we did. We read sex into every line. '*I set her on my pacing stead.* Come on, he sets her on his pacing stead!'

'Why doesn't he just say he set her on his *blue-veined throbbing love pump*, then?' That was the teacher. She treated us like the emerging adults we were. She knew we could appreciate a prurient joke without taking it to extremes. I loved those classes, where there was such trust.

'That was a good talk,' one of the sixteen-year-olds told me after the boys' Literature Dinner, 'but, to be honest, I really didn't quite understand when you went into the whole deep-psychological-analysing part.'

The 'deep psychological' stuff was what I took to be a simple analogy: a computer being overloaded and breaking down. And then it dawned on me that this student did not have an inordinate fear of failure. Quite a few of these boys did not understand what I knew the girls in their sister school felt, the deep-rooted terror at the pit of the stomach at the prospect of not doing well. Their questions were mostly practical: 'How did you get published, and what was it like?' And: 'How long did it take you to write your book?' 'This club was started by boys who loved reading,' one of them said, 'so what you see here are students who really want to be here.'

'Miz,' a boy yelled out in the middle of another presentation. 'Miz. What happened to your boyfriend in the book, miz?' The boys at Taylors Lakes Secondary College wanted to be here too, but only after twenty minutes, when they realised I wasn't going to theorise about issues of belonging and cross-cultural chasms. Watergardens is an area of Melbourne full of houses that seem to rise out of the ground like those in *Edward Scissorhands*, each of them trim and neat and seemingly under ten years old, like the high school. These kids wanted action. They wanted to know what happens next. 'Miz, what do you do now, miz?'

At a high school in regional Albury, I explained the Chinese-Cambodian saying from which my book title was derived: 'A girl is like cotton wool: once she's dirtied, she can never be clean again. A boy is like a gem: the more you polish it, the brighter it shines.' 'Hey, Kayla, would you like to polish my gem?' I heard a boy snickering after class.

But the girls at Hornsby Girls' High School, in outer Sydney, understood that I was not talking about wanking. Many of them had Asian faces, and told me about how differently they and their brothers were treated when they were growing up. Most people value the goose that lays the golden egg. But does it make a difference whether that goose is free-range or caged?

'Sometimes I feel like a human doing, not a human being,' wrote a student in a writing workshop I conducted. Another wrote about being one among a mass of 'sheeple'. It doesn't matter whether they are from public or private schools: young adults all seem to feel the same way sometimes.

The day I visited Shepherds Park School, in Wagga Wagga's juvenile-detention centre, I was entirely unprepared for the sight of the three-metre-high fence topped with closely wound spirals of barbed wire: what must these students have done to end up here? I was greeted at the front office by Simon, the principal, a convivial man whose face lacked the severity I had expected of the principal of such a place – or of any secondary school. I was also given a short induction by Graham, who worked in the front office. 'Now, we are allowed to restrain the kids by force, but they get a number of warnings before we do. So don't be alarmed if we have to hand-cuff them or tackle them to the floor. It doesn't happen very often when there is a guest, but be prepared.'

Can all of these boys read and write? I asked. 'Most of them can,' Tracy, an English teacher, told me, 'but some of them have very low literacy skills. And they would have covered that up at their schools by refusing to do any work in class and saying, '"That's just baby stuff. I know all that already."'

I walked into the classroom and noticed the locks on the door and windows. Then the boys filed in, slouchy-backed, monosyllabic. They looked just like boys I had met in so many other schools.

'What would you like to do? Would you like to do some writing work, or would you like me to just tell you a few stories?'

'Stories,' one murmured, and the rest grunted assent.

So I spent the next hour telling them funny stories that Dad told me, about surviving the Khmer Rouge, and the ingenious ways he had of finding food, of not getting killed. David Gilbey, a writer and a lecturer in English at Charles Sturt University, told me about his visits to the men's prison in nearby Junee. 'The men like seeing outsiders, people in normal society. They are thirsting to know that they can relate to "normal" people, so when I went to talk to the men in maximum security, they were very respectful.' And of all the schools I had visited in the past three years, I'd never had such attentive listeners. The boys gave me complete stillness for a full hour, and each came to shake my hand after the talk. They taught me more about expressing respect for a stranger than most of the other places with their blanket allegations of 'very interesting'.

The teacher's aide spoke to me later: 'You know, a lot of these kids come from very racist families. They've probably never had the experience of speaking to someone like you before.' It was a tiny school in a regional city, and these weren't free-range kids by any stretch of the imagination, but when I walked out of that wired enclosure, I wanted to walk straight back into Simon's office and apply for a job.

SHUNNED IN A
STRANGE LAND

Their big apartment blocks are like pointed middle fingers scraping the Melbourne skyline. Their presence in our city is only tolerated because they bring money into our education system. They are anti-social, rich young foreigners who 'form ghettos and don't assimilate'.

This is what is said about our international students, and these perceptions dangerously verge on the kind of racist rhetoric we thought had ended a decade ago. Worse, they are not true.

I worked for half a decade as a pastoral care adviser and residential tutor at the residential colleges of Melbourne University, in some of the most privileged academic environments. I have seen my students through the beginning of their degrees, when they are finding their feet in a foreign country, to their graduations and the quest for permanent residency. During this time, I have come to respect and admire their stoicism. They do not live in their own little worlds: they have opened up my world.

When they first arrive from countries such as China, India, Taiwan, Hong Kong, even as far away as Botswana, they are lonely and homesick. Feelings are the same in young adults everywhere: isolation, loneliness, the need for acceptance and respect.

Orientation week is daunting and international students soon start to become invisible, because they do not go to pubs twice a week. Drinking makes my local students garrulous and extroverted, qualities that seem to earn acceptance and respect in Australia but many international students come from cultures where drinking is not a social pastime.

When local students go off to the pub, the college is usually empty but for the international students. In the quiet spaces of the evenings, these students have taught me how to crochet, how to appreciate anime and moon-cakes with red-bean filling, and they talk to me about their parents back home. They shyly speak about how awkward it is to adapt to the shared unisex bathrooms, the heaviness of the meals, the loudness of the music.

Some have woken in the middle of the night with heart palpitations because they felt they were four years deep into studying the wrong course. But career counsellors did not listen to the silence between their words. 'Follow your heart' was their advice. Yet one of my students could not follow her heart lest it exploded. Her family had invested all their life-savings into her education and in return she was to study hard and obtain permanent residency, to bring her parents here for a better life. She could not switch courses; it was financially and logistically impossible. This young woman sought my counsel, but she taught me more about acceptance and stoicism than I could ever teach her.

There is a misconception that all international students are cashed-up because they pay the exorbitant fees that our government extracts from them. There is also the pointed accusation that international students do not 'assimilate', but this is not always a choice they are able to make. They do not 'form ghettos'; on the contrary, they are largely and deeply in our community, yet they are also largely ignored. They are the students who serve our meals in Chinatown, the people who drive our taxis. They are the lowest paid and often most exploited workers, unprotected by Australian workplace relations legislation. We refuse to see their toils because it does not accord with our image of how our overseas cash-calves should be.

Eventually, most find company and comfort in the presence of each other. No one seems to begrudge Western students latching on to other Westerners when studying in Asia and forming insular little expatriate communities to observe the locals as if they were sociological studies instead of people who are only separated by a different culture. But somehow, we in Australia seem to demand assimilation from our temporary visitors, instead of offering acceptance and understanding.

Many international students are acutely aware that their parents back home are breaking their backs and bank accounts to send them here. It is not their duty to assimilate: many of them come here, under no uncertain terms, for an education.

It is our duty to deliver that education, but perhaps it is also our obligation to show to our young overseas visitors that we are also a tolerant society, and that we see them.

IT'S TIME TO EMBRACE
THE 'F' WORD

No teacher likes to hear the 'F' word, particularly not during final-exam time. That's understandable: 'failure' seems frightening when students are constantly told that they are not limited by anything, and should excel at everything. A certain paradigm of success is encouraged, and a particular type of student is hailed as the consummate model to fulfil this ideal: the High-Achiever.

The High-Achiever is the perfect student because teachers have no need to upbraid her, only to encourage. If she ever struggles, she is asked to think of her tribulations as material for a potential book about her future glory. She is labelled a perfectionist, but that is not to be considered a term of derision. Conversely, she is taught to list it as her greatest flaw to land jobs in interviews. Yet although she may be accomplished at everything, there is one thing that the High-Achiever cannot handle: the dreaded 'f' word.

As a teacher, I am taught never to tell students they've failed, only that they 'did not pass'. Students are sensitive, we are told, and any shake to their self-esteem will shatter their desire to achieve. We are taught to teach our students how to succeed, but we never let them question why they should. Once during a school visit when I put that question up on a big overhead projector, an alarmed teacher asked whether I was telling students to fail.

But when I speak directly to high-school students they are curious, because they are braver and more resourceful than our society gives them credit for. Students realise that if we don't learn to have a good relationship with failure, but are just taught to doggedly work at success, then the terrible fear comes in. The fear of losing. The anxiety about not attaining. The conviction that your best is never good enough.

As a university pastoral care adviser, I know that often the High-Achiever is a person with severe anxiety problems. She will cry in the toilets if she gets an A instead of an A+. She will control her body in self-destructive ways, while the rampant fears in her mind are left unchecked. She may be the migrant who is studying at the library during lunchtimes because when she gets home she has to sew for her parents. Or she may be the middle-class model from Kew who coaches the debating team and runs a marathon. But often when she comes to see me, she is not a healthy person.

When I was seventeen, my teachers took me to a small and secret room within the labyrinth of school corridors, so that I could re-learn how to breathe. I had also lost the ability to remember when to eat, sleep and speak. Up until I 'lost it', society, my loved ones and well-intentioned people continued to reward the anxiety-ridden, petty-minded and unhappy person I was because my academic achievements appeared so impressive.

But there is nothing impressive about a nervous breakdown. No one wants to know you anymore. Your friends float into the periphery. You are like a useless machine that no longer works, a computer that has run too many programs, caught a virus and crashed. Who will use you for inspiration now, when no one wants to catch your disease? Dulled by depression, your rubber-mask of a face must not be seen, so you learn to hide yourself from the world. You are a cipher.

This is the other side of success – the risk of losing your resilience, courage and curiosity. At seventeen, I lost it to such a degree that I no longer cared whether I ate, slept or survived. This doesn't fit into a narrative of accomplishment.

This is the reason why I never focus on telling a tunnel-vision story of success to students. Not all of us will reach such dizzying heights. Yet all of us have experienced some degree of loneliness, loss, self-doubt and despair. We must learn how to deal with these very real matters first and foremost. We must realise that being successful will not eliminate these natural and inevitable feelings. We must realise this before these negative feelings become insurmountable. If you have cultivated an anxious, unhappy persona, it's harder to be happy merely because of a change in circumstances. In fact, any higher accomplishment will only breed more insecurities and anxieties, larger and more hideous than the last.

As our students sit their final exams, I hope they will give it their best shot and remember that what matters in the long run is not perfection, but perspective. When Sir Winston Churchill said that 'success consists of going from failure to failure without loss of enthusiasm', he had pretty good perspective. Let's hope that this is the kind of learning that is encouraged in our students.

THE SECRET LIFE OF THEM

Tina Huang, fifteen, is what the Victorian Department of Education and Early Childhood Development classifies as a 'gifted' child. The Year 9 student is undertaking the Select Entry Accelerated Learning (SEAL) program at Box Hill High School. Running in thirty-six government schools throughout the state, the program was designed to stem the flow of talented students from public to private education by creating an environment that would challenge and stimulate bright children. Students begin Year 8 work in Year 7, and can complete their secondary education in five years instead of six, or they can choose to undertake a more comprehensive Victorian Certificate of Education that takes three years instead of two.

Tina's parents were granted permanent Australian residency after the 1989 Tiananmen Square massacre in Beijing. With a university degree apiece, the Huangs wanted to give their future children, Tina and her younger sister Nicole, a better life in Australia. They bought a small business, Mussel's Fish and Chippery, across the road from Tina's Catholic primary school at the end of a short ribbon of boutique cafes and gift shops in Elwood. London plane trees dapple the enormous Edwardian and Queen Anne–style houses with shade and lend the neighbourhood an ambience of class and continuity, but for a concrete block of rental flats. 'That's where we used to live,' Tina says, pointing to one of the balconies jutting from the building.

The beach is a few minutes' walk away, but Tina never went there much. She just wasn't interested – hers was not that kind of childhood. Primary school plays and concerts were seen as indulgences; Tina rarely took part. Every weekend, her parents would drive the thirty-five minutes to the Asian stores in Springvale, in Melbourne's south-east, to buy cheap groceries. When her mum and dad were not working, they were usually sleeping, because their shop was open till late. Tina would clean, or watch over her little sister, or practise doing sums. Her parents drilled into her that maths was the most important subject. Maths made sense, particularly in their shop. When Tina was asked at school to write about her weekend, her parents wondered what on earth the school was teaching her, not fathoming that in the surrounding brick houses, children's lives ruled entire Saturdays and Sundays. 'Looking back, I sort of get why other kids gave me such a hard time,' Tina says. 'I was an unforgiving, obnoxious brat who didn't think much of creative writing or playing around.'

'When I was about five,' she tells me, 'family friends came over, and their daughter had got into MacRobertson Girls' High School. From then on, that was what my parents kind of expected of me too.' Tina's mum and dad understood it to be a good school because it required students to pass an entrance examination; only the smartest students were sifted through. Also, it was a government school, which meant education was essentially free.

Tina's extracurricular activities promptly became curricular. She had always been a bright child, but her parents believed she could be further ahead than she was. Soon, she was spending most of her free hours in after-school tutoring, including on weekends and during school holidays. At this early age, none of it was her choice, and the extra work set her apart from her schoolmates. It also instilled in her the idea that time had to be 'used constructively'.

At age ten, Tina was enrolled at a popular coaching college, one with more than forty branches across Australia. Every Thursday after school, Tina would take a three-hour scholarship-preparation class. 'I sat in a classroom and did a maths and an English test, followed by two writing pieces,' Tina explains. 'For an extra $25 you could also do an abstract-reasoning test. They run the tests through a machine and *tah-dah*, you have your results and self-worth all summed up in a pretty blue graph.'

There are now hundreds of such colleges around Australia, dedicated to drilling students in the skills needed to win scholarships to private schools, to get into selective state schools like MacRobertson or North Sydney Boys High, or to gain admission to state schools' SEAL programs. These coaching colleges do not require any form of certification from state educational departments and are free to set their own curricula. The more successful companies, such as James An College, have many satellite offices in suburbs where there is a high concentration of Asian parents, many of whom, like Tina's, work long hours, putting their earnings into their kids' education. Courses are often booked out months ahead. The companies kill two birds with one stone: not only do they alleviate the guilt parents face at leaving their kids at home alone for long stretches, they also make that 'idle' time productive.

I went to an information night held by one such college. When I phoned beforehand, I was advised the company did not teach 'generalised maths and English skills', but focused on 'techniques for taking scholarship or selective entry – school examinations'. The session took place on a Sunday evening in the small hall of a leafy primary school. On arrival I was handed a clipboard, a stack of papers, a highlighter and a red pen, then told to take a seat.

There were five Chinese and Indian families. With the exception of a boy and girl in Year 8, the children were in Years 3 to 5. The three Caucasian attendees had come without their children.

The woman who gave the presentation (and ran the company) had the demeanour of the kind of old-fashioned school mistress who would post the results of every student on the board at the end of each week. She spoke as if addressing a much larger audience and urged parents to find schools that filtered the brightest students from the rest. She singled out a small Catholic school in the outer-eastern suburbs, which one of the Indian children, a shy girl, was attending in the hope of winning a Year 9 scholarship to a private school. 'Half the numbers in this school,' the presenter said, not hiding her sarcasm, 'are studying vocational education subjects: *fascinating* subjects like *horse studies*.' One of the mothers laughed loudly.

The presenter asked the Year 8 boy which maths book he was using in class, then told him he was already lagging behind because the SEAL students at state schools were studying Year 9 maths. She mentioned how some schools wanted 'well-rounded' students who were engaged with their communities, and advised parents that they could get around this by finding a topical issue in their local paper and getting their child to write a letter to the council opposing the cutting down of a tree or the installation of new poker machines. The letter could then be included in the student's portfolio should they get an interview with a school. She told us there was 'no need to lock little Johnny up in a room all afternoon, forcing him to read about the war in Sudan' because scholarship tests do not cover foreign affairs or ethical issues. She knew the details of each company that administered tests for the different schools, the contents of past tests and exactly how many students had sat for each one. Again and again, the same mother hooted with glee: she had clearly found herself a kindred spirit. No pain, no gain.

Near the end of the session, the presenter put up slides with sample multiple-choice questions from previous exams for us to answer. One asked us to measure the amount of liquid in a vial if two-thirds of it was poured into a different jar. Another question had us pick out the antonym of an archaic word. Finally, the presenter reminded parents that before a student embarked on this month-long program of practice tests, her company offered a three-and-a-half-hour pre-practice test – at a cost of $150 – to judge whether the child should even bother.

'The scholarship classes I took were soul-crushing,' says Tina. 'A coaching college! Dude, there are five-year-olds walking around that place. What are you possibly *coaching* them?' Still, Tina muses: 'I am yet to meet an Asian child who doesn't do some form of consistent tutoring.'

*

After years of preparation, Tina sat the various entrance examinations for selective state high schools, private schools offering scholarships and schools offering accelerated education programs. She was eight, nine, ten, then eleven. That time now seems a blur to Tina. Each year rolled by in vain. The entrance exams usually took place on a Saturday morning or afternoon, and the women and men in the community – the small-business vendors and managers and migrants with dormant university degrees, as well as the factory workers and at-home sewing-machine operators with their Year 4 educations – sent their sons and daughters along to these exams.

Raised in a culture that since 605 AD has employed a merit-based civil-service examination system to reward academic excellence with tangible, life-changing consequences, many Chinese-Australian parents understand education as a way to shift class. With insufficient time, energy or resources to change their own circumstances, first-generation migrant parents generally encourage their children to work within the system. This has led to the almost exclusive emphasis on examination results, and often leaves the entire burden on the small shoulders of the students themselves. (When I was thirteen, my parents hired a maths tutor for a month to help me pass the test to get into MacRobertson, the only selective girls' state high school in Victoria. I did not get in.)

At the age of fourteen, instead of visiting friends or holding slumber parties, Tina spent a few weeks sitting in scholarship coaching classes after school, to 'test them out' for her younger sister, who was in Year 5. 'I didn't want her to go through the same awful experience I did,' she explains.

'I didn't get into MacRob. I didn't get into a private school through a scholarship. None of them.'

Instead, Tina made it into the SEAL program at Box Hill High, and she is flourishing. She has joined the debating team, become class captain and even taken a creative-writing class. Earlier this year, when the class was asked to write about a piece of creative nonfiction, Tina chose the Gospels. Her teacher, Imogen Melgaard, tells me, 'Tina's intellect is frightening sometimes, because it is so easy to forget that she is only a kid. At times I have to stop myself from speaking to her like she's an adult and my equal.'

Each SEAL school is responsible for determining its own selection criteria, which means students are not siphoned off by a single test. The inclusion of interviews and Year 6 reports means that the SEAL program takes a broader approach to determining which students to admit. Their personalities and characters matter. Melgaard notes that SEAL students feel a level of acceptance here that might be absent if they'd remained in ordinary classes: 'They would be the one or two kids who would stand out and be picked on. But here, they have their *Doctor Who* club and their chess club, and they bring textbooks to school camps. There is a strong culture of pride in doing well.'

Half of Melgaard's SEAL class is Asian. She remarks that 'it is fascinating how much Asian pride these kids have. They will joke to me about the "Asian Five" subjects that students study for VCE' – two maths, physics, chemistry and English – 'and also about the "Asian fail", which is an A-minus'.

Box Hill High used to be a working-class boys college. But its SEAL program has done more than just revitalise the school; it has helped change the demographics of a suburb. In 1996, the median house price in Box Hill was $150,000. Yet as more and more parents moved to be within the school zone, property prices soared. In 2001, the median house price was $280,000. Ten years later it was $960,000.

Now when you emerge from Box Hill's train station, 14 kilometres east of Melbourne's CBD, you step into a shopping mall that would not look out of place in Singapore. There is a Giordano store selling polo shirts in every conceivable bright colour, and well-made pants in conservative cuts. There are Chinese cake shops and bubble tea outlets, and the whole centre gleams Domestos-white. Youths wear flip-flops down the street, but they wear them with designer jeans.

Beyond Box Hill Centro lies an inner-city foodie's dream – stretches of dumpling restaurants and kopitiams. The largest group of overseas-born residents in Box Hill is from mainland China. Almost all shopfronts have signage in Chinese, in addition to English. It is said, half-jokingly among Asians here, that a person could live in Box Hill and never have to deal with the English-speaking populace: they could shop, eat, bank and even bury their loved ones in their own dialect. It was recently expressed in more charged terms through a now-banned Facebook page called

'Playing "Spot the Aussie" in Box Hill'. While it was up, the Facebook page was liked by nearly 12,000 people, many of whom posted rants about unhygienic, job-stealing, unassimilated Asians.

One thing is clear, though – there is a sense of community. The new migrants in Box Hill have added an air of cosmopolitan sophistication. Restaurants now open later at night, and the eating strip near Whitehorse Road teems with families and fast patter. For new arrivals seeking manual or market work, this is where you can make connections and find out where to send your kids to school. Lined woollen blazers, alumni networks and new swimming pools don't mean much to people who might have been in this country for only a handful of years, but they're quick to switch to a system that boasts the greatest number of graduates to top universities, or the highest Australian Tertiary Admissions Rankings.

Recently, Tina was invited to talk at Melbourne University about the SEAL program to a postgraduate class studying 'gifted education'. 'I was a SEAL student for three years before my mum heard my speech and went, "Oh, so that's what you're doing, Tina. Well, good luck. Is that why everyone else is doing it?"'

*

At the Box Hill library, I meet Tina's friend and classmate Aaron, who is sixteen. He lives locally but, like Tina, does not go out much. After school, he walks his three younger sisters home, prepares some food for them and returns to his studies. Aaron's father, an engineer, arrived in Australia in the early 1980s from Vietnam, and his mother migrated two years later. They moved to Box Hill after hearing about the local SEAL program.

Aaron is shy. He wants to become a corporate lawyer. Asked why, he replies he's keen on 'security'. 'Are you happy?' I ask him. He looks at me for a long moment before replying: 'What is happiness?'

'You know it when you feel it,' I suggest.

No, it's more complicated than that, Aaron insists. 'It's different for everyone.' Happiness, he tells me, has a lot to do with security.

Aaron keeps glancing to check on his sisters, who are also at the library. At the back are small carrels — tiny rooms where a person can sequester themselves all afternoon to study. On the library noticeboard, in addition to flyers for the Henry Lawson society and Chinese-language classes on internet use, there is an advertisement for a parents' forum on 'supporting stressed, anxious or depressed teenagers'.

*

Tina and I are walking down her favourite running track. 'I hate running,' she tells me, 'but it makes me feel good afterwards.' We are in her new suburb. Her parents moved to Balwyn so that Nicole would be within the catchment zone of Balwyn High School, which also has a SEAL program and whose students regularly top the state's Year 12 results. The family relocated their Elwood fish-and-chip shop, where business was good, to The Happy Snapper in Canterbury, closer to where they now live. Meanwhile, Tina continues to commute to Box Hill.

I ask her what she is most afraid of.

'Failure,' she answers instantly.

'But when was the last time you failed?'

'Does burning toast in the morning count?' Then she says, 'I think the fear comes from not being able to come back from being stuck in a horrible place.'

On the day of Tina's Year 12 biology exam, she is hyperventilating and breathing into a paper bag. (At the end of Year 8, twenty-five of the seventy-five SEAL students at Tina's school are selected to study a VCE science subject. 'So I'm like the accelerated of the accelerated,' she tells me.) Confessing that she gets sick after every exam, to the point where she has to take antibiotics, Tina tells me that this one is particularly nerve-racking because the marks count towards her Australian Tertiary Admission Rank. To prepare, Tina has completed fifty practice biology exams – 150 hours' worth. She sourced the practice exams from teachers, tutors and friends, and bought more online.

Over the six months I spend getting to know her, Tina's self-esteem seems precariously balanced between soaring confidence and debilitating anxiety. This is the price paid by a constantly coached student: underneath all that stoicism, there is a quiet resentment at being forced into a system that judges you by very narrow parameters.

Even private schools are beginning to acknowledge that a coached student may not necessarily have the type of rounded, inquisitive mind they are after. Sydney Grammar School, for instance, strongly discourages academic coaching as preparation for its scholarship exam. If the purpose behind education for the gifted is to ensure that the brightest students are sufficiently challenged, then this idea of extra, relentless tutoring cranks the dial all the way back around to the beginning, where naturally curious intellects are no longer being challenged in the ways that matter, and students' skills are limited to test-taking and thinking within the rules.

Indeed, when Julia Gillard declared that the Asian Century begins in the classroom, coaching colleges were hardly what she meant. Amy Chua's controversial book *Battle Hymn of the Tiger Mother* raised an unsettling question about education: is giftedness inherent, or is it all about the hard slog? Asian cities such as Shanghai may top OECD charts for educational attainment, but many teachers in Australia are sceptical about whether the rigid, rote-learning techniques used there will create the sort of adaptive and flexible future workers and leaders needed in the decades ahead.

My last meeting with Tina takes place inside a McDonald's in Balwyn. She tells me about her sister, Nicole. Tina's careful scoping exercise for a suitable coaching college eventually yielded the same one that hosted the information session I attended. 'It cost $2000 for a month, and Nicole cried every week of that month,' Tina confesses. 'But it worked.' So much so, that Tina's sister didn't even end up going to Balwyn High, the school that was the reason for their parents' relocation. Nicole won a scholarship to Camberwell Girls Grammar School, which has annual fees of around $20,000. 'She did better than me,' says Tina with a half-laugh, half-sigh. Then she is pensive. 'You know, I've never really met any Asian parents who believe the whole "not everything that counts can be counted" thing,' she says. 'But I have that phrase plastered next to the "How to Succeed in Year 12 Biology" sheets on my wall. It keeps me sane.'

LETTER TO A

You ripped down the wallpaper one day when you were fourteen, ripped it right off the walls, all four of them, and then stuck up posters all over the room to hide the scabby paint. One day it will get painted over, you told yourself. One day the broken window will get fixed. One day the carpets will get changed. One day the ceiling will not fall down. One day the cracks will not be there, one day the smell will not be there, and when that day comes you will be out. Out of there. You will not be there to see it all. One day you will be out of there and one day you will live a freshly white-washed life. Yes you will, and the ceiling will no longer peel and fall on top of you and these four walls will no longer close in on you, and you will have cauterised your wants.

There is a depression in the wall. These depressions come about when your knuckles itch and your upper deltoids ache to exert themselves and your mind is nothing but a blank black hole screaming to see red, that is when you strike and don't think of the consequences. This is when your inarticulate rage causes you to bunch up your fist and punch the wall so hard that the clock falls down on the other side, since there is no one to listen to your choked half-finished sentences about a cousin, a cousin who was once like a brother but is now nothing more than crap for all you care, a cousin so far gone that you don't think of the money he has borrowed from you or the money he owes you, the money to get out, you do not think about it at all because you do not want to think about him. To think about him is to stumble down the path of despair and once you are on that path, you have to keep running, keep running or else if you stop and pause to see what direction you are going, you will sink to your knees and realise how much you need water, water like the water bottles they carry down the streets of Richmond, and you can always tell which ones are the ones on the habit because of these water bottles.

We were powerpoints, powerpoints with the three holes, two that slanted upwards and one that was a straight stroke down, straight and narrow and sad, like the prospect of some of us spending the rest of our lives doing PowerPoint presentations because our names are Andrew Chan and we wear glasses and sit in front of our PCs after school each evening because our parents want us to study hard and become successful, because this is a land of great opportunity and we must not waste it, it is a land of great fairness where even Ah Chan selling BanCao at the market in Saigon can raise a son who can decipher strange symbols in front of a screen merely by pressing many buttons in different combinations on a black pad, and it assures him to hear the clackity clack noise like an old abacus coming from his son's room, because then he knows that his son knows more than he does. Old Ah Chan doesn't have a clue about what the information superhighway is, all he knows is that there are no casualties, none at all, and that it can only go up from here. And so he buys his son the magic machine with the clopclop buttons and with a few clackity clacks and clicks he can transport himself to a nice office and a house in the suburbs and a shiny new blue Mazda.

Chink is an insult, but chink is also the sound that money makes as it rattles in your father's pockets, it is also the sound that those machines at the casino make when he hits the jackpot, so chink is not necessarily too bad a word. Chink is the only word that governs the life of your father, chink chink chink of the coins in the gaming machine, chink chink chink one at a time and not all at once, and so he sits there to wait for the sound of all-at-once chinks, meanwhile at home the boy and the mother and the kid brother sit together for a dinner of rice and vegetables and bits of beef before parting to play computer games or watch Chinese serials in separate rooms. You go off to your room and turn up the music, real loud music, and you look at the white wall which you had determined to paint a mural on, 'cause your art teacher says that you have real talent, but what the hell, what now? What is determination now, when the father won't come back and when the father won't stop spending the money and won't stop believing in the glorious sound of the chinkchinkchink of the machine.

A steady beat of chinks from the coins in his pocket, waiting for the rapid succession of chinkchinkchinks like the quickening of a heartbeat until the glorious rushing sound cannot be separated into its individual tinkles but all pours forth like a mad gold rush.

This is a different gold rush from the gold rush of the nineteenth century when we men had to carry heavy buckets and sift away to find the little pieces, and we needed strong stomachs to swallow the pieces and keen eyes to sift through the processes of our digestive tracts to find that little hard lump.

Meanwhile, swallow that lump in your throat you big sook, 'cause big boys aren't sooks goddam it, and look at your comic books and pictures of *Dragonball Z* and pick up the phone to call the number of that little pale-faced girl with the dark eyes and the black hair, even if she makes you write her letters instead of wanting to talk in person. Let the phone ring and ring and goddam is there anyone home? Keep your finger on the little soft grey 'off' button on the cordless phone in case her parents pick up and interrogate you worse than those Mao guards during the bloody cultural revolution that would not leave your family alone, that sent them to Vietnam, and then to this new land where little white-faced girls with black hair laugh at your stories of killing chickens in the Guangzhou countryside, and all your history becomes a funny after-dinner anecdote. Others would see your acts as barbaric, and squeeze their clean faces into squished looks of shudder-shake – 'eww, how gross' – even as they are seated opposite you eating a McChicken burger or severing the joints of the skinny bones of KFC chicken wings with shiny fingers.

And so you lie on your bed in your room waiting for the father to come home, and you can hear the sound of your mother's footsteps padding to the kitchen to wash the dishes from dinner. You sit up and decide to write the girl a letter, a poem even, although you know all of this means nothing to you even though the girl means something to you, little ivory-faced girl in a tower. Grab a few sheets of Reflex paper, A4, nothing fancy. Goddam if the girl is expecting perfumed notepaper, well this was the best she was going to get and she had better be happy with it. Bloody hell, how are you going to do this when you couldn't give a damn about this decomposed Keats your English teacher keeps mentioning?

Words are there to convey action, not an endless quagmire of feelings, and whatever you are feeling is transformed into action. And that is why, for the life of you, you can't understand why the girl will not go out with you and all she wants to do is to write these bloody letters to you and wants you to write these bloody letters back to her. The surest way to get to know a person is to meet them, and take them out in your car with your recently attained Ps, God you are proud of these plates, and ask her questions but not too many, and do something fun like going to a movie or something.

But this girl, she's a strange girl. You wonder whether you should pursue her, whether this stupid poem will persuade her to actually go out with you. Grant you that date so you can be with someone for once and not have to say a word and just forget about things and have fun. But this girl, this girl looks like she can't have fun. Something about the look in her eyes, as if she is a little scared of what she sees in the world around her. Like she spends a lot of time thinking about why it is all so terrifying, and keeping quiet about her answers. You have no time for enigmas, you want to get out there and get some action, although not necessarily from this girl, because she is a good girl. You are sick to death of sitting still, of doing nothing.

You pick up the phone again and dial the number of the girl. 'Hello?' Ah, the familiar voice, you can imagine her now, sitting at her desk, which is where you imagine her to be, if you are not imagining her in other more pleasant places that suit your fancy but probably not her reality. You have called to chat to get your mind off things, but she does not want to chat, this girl. She wants to talk, goddam it why is it that the stereotype is true, why do women always want to talk about feelings and shit as if these feelings will change anything?

Ding-dong. That's the bell. The father is home, the mother must be lying in bed, wide awake. You swear you can almost hear the bedsprings creak as she gets up. Creak creak. You can certainly hear the footsteps, the creak creak snap snap of the tendons of her feet and ankles as she shuffles to the door. You wonder whether the little brother is asleep, and whether he is going to wake up this evening. You wait to hear the inevitable question. 'Where have you been?' Even though your mother knows the answer she asks it anyway.

She can see the chinkchinkchink in his eyes, see the bags beneath. Dark bags beneath carrying phantasmagoric gold coins.

He blinks once or twice, and the illusion is gone. He is tired. So tired. The bags hang down to his cheekbones, they become bags of bones, he is a bag of bones. 'How much did you use?' your mother demands. 'How much did you lose?' The terms are interchangeable, and it doesn't matter which one comes out.

'I'm hungry, woman, haven't had dinner yet,' the sad man in the old brown leather jacket with the elastic at the bottom grumbles.

'If you came home earlier, you wouldn't have to eat leftovers,' grumbles the mother, as she shuffles to the kitchen, but she brings out the beef from the stove, the beef she would not let you eat too much of because she was saving it for him.

AGAINST CALAMITOUS ODDS

I first came across the work of Ruth Park in primary school. There was something viscerally real about the olden-day world of *Playing Beatie Bow*. I couldn't properly understand it – but, looking back now, I realise that the power of 'Sydney's Dickens' lay in her ability to write about love, sex and death with an innocence unmarred by adult stigmas.

Swords and Crowns and Rings was published in 1977, not long before *Playing Beatie Bow*, and it won the Miles Franklin Award. The saga takes place in the first three decades of the twentieth century, and like Park's much-loved novels of the late 1940s, *Harp in the South* and *Poor Man's Orange*, it's about the stoic poor. Yet there is a shift from the deep-rooted sense of community in her earlier books, set in the slums of inner-city Sydney, to Jackie Hanna and Cushie Moy's quest for individual self-realisation. While Park does not inch from portraying stark privation, this novel marks the beginning of a new, transcendental consciousness in her characters.

Propelled by their Tolkien-like search for a kingdom of dwarves who make 'swords and crowns and rings', Jackie and Cushie share an enchanted childhood. They are completely unselfconscious, and so are complete – 'they had always been two sides of the same coin: she, in her physical perfection and defencelessness, like a beautiful gentle bird, he so small and grotesque, and yet hardy, full of purpose.'

When their united sense of self is shattered by forced separation, they endure almost a decade apart from each other. Like the Buddhist symbol of the lotus, whose roots grip the bottom of the muddy swamp but whose head rises cleanly above the water, though, Park's protagonists accept life's vicissitudes. They suffer the slings and arrows of outrageous fortune, but their most profound journey is to maintain their integrity against calamitous odds.

This allegorical journey of emerging adulthood came out of a period of great social and political change. Influenced by the Civil Rights Movement in the United States, Australia saw the passage of the first equal-opportunity legislation in 1975. Diversity was no longer quashed by assimilationist policies – it was becoming the nation's new narrative. The character of Jackie could be nuanced and human without needing to represent difference.

Park had by this time abandoned the Catholic faith of her youth and become interested in Zen Buddhism. She had also seen some of the world beyond the antipodes since the publication of her last major novel, in 1957. *Swords and Crowns and Rings* was her return to publishing for adults after spending the previous two decades predominantly writing children's books and radio plays. When Park sat down to write about Jackie and Cushie, she was no longer dealing with fixed absolutes but with fluid, more radical identities.

The prostitutes and derelicts, the homeless men and indigent immigrant farming women who epitomise Park's gritty realism still populate this book; but there is also a pair of affectionate quarrelsome women lovers, Claudie and Iris, and a victim of violence and incest, who becomes one of the strongest figures in the novel. Most strikingly, the protagonist, whose presence would cause discomfort and antagonism in a time of ignorance and poverty, is always rendered with dignity. Jackie is not a quirk of a man but manhood at its best. His identity is forged through unemployment, physical violence and the Depression.

The gentle irony in this expansive novel is that garrulousness is seen as a flaw, and the deepest characters are those who do not speak much: the Nun, Lufa, the magisterial ailing German grandfather. These are solitary men whose lives run slowly, on self-sustaining cogs, and their actions render them substantial. 'Probably I am a writer because I had a singular childhood,' Park once wrote. 'My first seven years I spent all alone in the forest, like a possum or bear cub.' She did not grow up in a household full of books, instead learning to be an astute eavesdropper and an observer of the human condition. The characters that fascinated her most were those with eccentricities, their faces lined with the calligraphic marks of experience.

Park set much of *Swords and Crowns and Rings* in rural Australia, a reticent place where folk have no need to vocalise every thought that passes through their minds. 'I saw a little of this vast, magnificent land, and was captured forever by its noble indifference to humankind,' she observed. 'I felt that one day this continent would give a shrug and shake all the humans off into the sea. But it would still be its own self. That's what I call identity.'

The characters' external surrounds mirror their internal universes: Jackie's strength and resilience are as immutable as the inviolate land from which he comes, while Cushie is as soft and beautiful as her artificial environment, where the family wealth perches on a precipice, liable at any time to fall. Cushie, ostensibly so lamblike, is essential to Jackie's developing sense of manhood. Unsure about the parameters of her existence, uncertain where the world ends and she begins, Cushie is constantly bumping up against sharp corners. Jackie is not so troubled: he has a role model of noble, good-humoured masculinity, the Nun; and the love of a strong woman, his mother. Cushie's glacial mother, Isobel, and her inwardly cowering father impose silence in the house – silence born not of dignity but fear. A young woman of infinite faith and utter dependency, Cushie has femininity imposed upon her; she is trapped by it, despite her attempts to gain control.

Maida, on the other hand, is Jelka Sepic in John Steinbeck's story 'The Murder' rendered three-dimensional, with agency and a voice. Stronger and more courageous than Cushie, she suffers vicious cruelty but remains tender and kind. She did not grow up in refinement, yet maintains a sense of quiet self-respect, as Jackie notices: 'he became aware that Maida had a little bag of herbs around her neck on a string, and he was touched at this fastidiousness in one whose life was so isolated and austere.' Maida is egoless, never having had the chance to choose, to develop her own identity. A cornered creature on the cruel family farm, she can only make small gestures of kindness without considering the consequences.

Jackie knows a handful of people through his life, Cushie's world is conned to her family, Maida's is even smaller; yet these are people for whom love is not a mere feeling but a verb, and for this reason they are unforgettable. In the end, innocence, identity and integrity all lead back to the same thing, expressed by Cushie Moy as a child: 'Deep and true in her soul she knew only that she believed in loving, and all denial of this was dishonour.'

DARK FICTION

When Little Saigon Market in Footscray burned down, thousands of high-school textbooks burned as well. The books were donated to Les Twentyman's Back to School Program for disadvantaged students, and kept in an upstairs storeroom that sometimes sheltered homeless women.

Before that, they were housed in the same place as a methadone dispensary for recovering heroin addicts: a single room with couches and a little shrine my friend Richard, a social worker, had lovingly set up, adorned with photos of young people who'd died either from drug overdoses or gang violence, all of whom he knew by name. Teenagers who needed school books would walk up the flight of concrete steps and find their Kafka or S.E. Hinton on the shelves.

This was my neighbourhood, and my dad's electrical appliance shop was right next door. My parents never 'policed' the books I read – my mother couldn't read or write, and my father was just pleased to see us reading books. In Year 9, we studied *So Much to Tell You*, John Marsden's book about a selectively mute, traumatised Australian whose face had been disfigured by her father. Marina was honest, not chipper; often depressed, painfully self-conscious and slow to react. This book was narrated by a fourteen-year-old girl, and we were fourteen when we read it.

Our teacher, Ms Bonnie Clarke, imbued us with confidence, humour and a conviction to keep our own diaries.

When Marsden's *Tomorrow When the War Began* series came out, even kids who were proud non-readers devoured these books. Only as an adult and author did I realise, with surprise, what some teachers thought of the series: too much gratuitous violence and sex, filled with 'weak' adult characters and 'too-simplistic' prose. As a teenage child of refugees, I'd grown up with friends who'd actually survived real wars, and with parents who'd suffered from the same PTSD that Marsden wrote about with great insight and clarity. The weak or absent adult characters – which Marsden also balanced with kind and courageous adults – were just part of a humanity we understood. Some of my mates came to Australia as unaccompanied minors, and many of us had already suffered the indignation of adult racism at some point in our lives.

Often, stories about children and young adults are an 'adults-only' fantasy of childhood. They are usually written by adults, revealing more about the writer and their projections than the truth of their subjects. Whenever the debate about 'darkness' in books for children and young adults re-emerges, we get the same wearying responses about the malleability of children's minds, or how dark books may be redeemed by the inclusion of supervisory 'good' adult characters (such as in *Harry Potter*), and/or a 'good' message at the end (racism defeated; empathy for refugees resurrected).

This is because those most often asked to participate in this debate come from a very select group. Usually writers themselves, they are accustomed to giving their opinions, and have very specific ideas of what childhood or adulthood should be. They also generally come from literate, middle-income households with children who are physically safe, which is why the debate sounds frustratingly repetitive throughout the decades. It's all ideological, and ideology – no matter how benign or aspirational – can be damaging if it is far removed from the lived experiences of actual, real teenagers.

A few years ago, when I was asked at a girls school to talk about the killing fields, I received a gentle reminder not to go into too much gory detail lest I distress the Year 9s who were 'not ready for that kind of thing'. What kind of thing? I wondered. The kids a couple of suburbs down in the commission flats? The scholarship girl from Sudan sitting two seats away from them?

The publishing industry, schools and libraries are filled with benign and progressive people who care about inculcating children with the 'right' values, and instilling love, hope and kindness. As these people are also the ultimate decision-makers regarding what kids read – or what they don't – they often unwittingly convey to poorer students their class values of what constitutes 'good litera-ture' and 'bad morals'. There's a difference between rubbing a child's nose in *Game of Thrones* gore and violence and teaching them imaginative empathy about how different teenagers live, speak and experience the world – teenagers their own kids could easily know and befriend if they were allowed to catch the train two stops down.

Perhaps that's why some teachers who have no problem with teaching Shakespeare (murder, suicide, anti-Semitism, madness) baulk at touching anything by Sonya Hartnett or John Marsden. Perhaps there's the erroneous belief that young-adult writing is 'low-class', not the highbrow stuff of literary analysis.

Or maybe the teenagers in those books are too real, too vis-ceral. Perhaps a book about an acid attack on a teenage girl would be worthy and teachable if set in India or Cambodia, where the focus could be on misogyny in different cultures; but for Marsden to have set his seminal work at an Australian girls school was a huge risk. It paid off, because enlightened teachers like Ms Clarke taught it, and in doing so taught us that a teenage girl can be funny, sardonic and insightful without having to mimic middle-aged Henry James or Edith Wharton.

I can think of no better environment to read *The Hunger Games* or the *Tomorrow* series than in a school, guided by a teacher who can lead discussions about morality, courage and violence. After all, if fifteen-year-olds are studying *Heart of Darkness*, why draw the line at stories that might involve them as protagonists who might have to face difficult decisions earlier than adults anticipate or imagine?

Teenagers nudging past heroin-dependent adults to get to their books are not a reality we want to face, but this isn't the work of Dickensian fiction either. To say that stories about their gritty lived realities don't matter, are exaggerated or unworthy of careful consideration is to do these young adults a great disservice. To say that such stories might corrupt the more 'pure' minds of their more fortunate peers is patronising.

Gayle Forman, the popular American young-adult author, wrote: 'A novel won't turn a bookish drama geek into a promiscuous drug abuser any more than it will turn a promiscuous drug abuser into a bookish drama geek, unless the seeds of those transformations were already planted.' But it might help a young person recognise their life, and understand that their experiences are not invisible, that they matter.

CLOSE TO HOME

THE FLASHING
GREEN MAN

I began my story in a suburb of Melbourne, Australia, in a market swarming with fat pigs and thin people. The fat pigs are hanging from hooks, waiting to be hacked into segments, and the thin people are waiting to buy these segments wrapped in newspaper over a glass counter. When they haggle over the price of trotters, there is much gesticulating and furrowing of brow because the parties do not spick da Ingish velly good. 'Like a chicken trying to talk to a duck,' my mother calls these conversations. But she is not here today to quack over quality pigs' paws, because she is lying in a white hospital room waiting for me to arrive.

So it's just my father, standing smack-bang in the middle of this market, and his shoes are getting wet because of the blood diluted in the water that comes from the huge hoses used to wash away the mess at the end of the day. He looks down at the grates and thinks about pig's blood jelly and whether he'll ever buy it again. He likes the taste, but Ah Ung told him that he worked in the abattoir when he first came here and the carcasses were hung from hooks with buckets beneath to collect the pigs' blood. Because they were not washed properly, they would sometimes leak with piss and other filthy drips. My father does not think back to Phnom Penh, where he would be eating brains in broth made by street vendors stationed across the road from the homeless leper coughing out half a lung in the doorway of some derelict shopfront, but looks up and points at the pink and red appendages behind the glass. With his other hand, he holds up two fingers.

This is the suburb where words like 'and', 'at' and 'of' are redundant, where full sentences are not necessary. 'Two kilo dis. Give me seven dat.' If you were to ask politely, 'Would you please be so kind as to give me a half-kilo of the lady fingers?' the shop owner might not understand you. 'You wanna dis one? Dis banana? How many you want hah?' To communicate, my father realises, does not merely mean the strumming and humming of vocal cords, but much movement of hands and contortion of face. The loudest pokers always win, and the loudest pokers are usually women. My father's moment is lost when a middle-aged woman with Maggi-noodle curls points at the man behind the counter with a flailing forefinger and almost jabs out an eye as she accuses the other Non-English-Speaking Person of selling her furry trotters. 'Why yu gib me dis one? Dis one no good! Hairy here, here and dere! Hairy everywhere! Dat nother one over dere better. Who you save da nother one for hah?' Bang on the counter goes the bag of bloodied body parts, and my father knows that now is the time to scoot away to the stall opposite if he wants hairless ham.

This suburb has possibly the loudest and grottiest market in the Western world, although that term doesn't mean much when you're surrounded by brown faces. Footscray Market is the only market where you can peel and eat a whole mandarin before deciding whether to buy a kilo; where you can poke and prod holes in a mango to check its sweetness. My father does not even bat an eye at the kid who is covering her face with one hand, holding out a wet peeled lychee with the other, and wailing 'Aaarghhh! My eyeball!' to her little brother. He watches as the baby in the pram starts howling and the mother pulls off some grapes from a stand to shut him up while she goes on with her poking and prodding and justified pilfering. Parsimonious women aren't going to spend $4 on sour strawberries simply because they were too stupid to taste-test them first. 'Cause you more trouble coming back the second time!' declares my mother. 'Ayyah, no good to be tormented by $4! Try and avoid it if you can.' But there is no way to taste-test these trotters, my father thinks, as he looks through the clear plastic bag, so he has to take the word of the shouting woman in the opposite stall. He will bring these trotters home for his sister to boil into a broth, and then he will take the broth to the hospital for his wife.

He steps out onto the footpath, away from the damp smells of the market. He presses the black rubber button on the traffic lights and remembers when they first encountered these ticking poles.

Back where my father came from, cars did not give way to people, people gave way to cars. To have a car in Cambodia you had to be rich. And if you had money, it meant that you could drive at whatever speed you pleased. If the driver zipping down the country road accidentally knocked over a peasant farmer, he knew he had better zoom away quick because the whole village might come and attack him with cleavers. The little green man was an eternal symbol of government existing to serve and protect. And any country that could have a little green flashing man was benign and wealthy beyond imagining.

UNPOLISHED GEM

'Ah Bukien wants to discuss Aghere for her son,' my mother announced to my father over breakfast one morning. They spoke as if I wasn't there, but they expected me to eavesdrop. This woman, a family friend of my parents, had been intent on seeing me marry her son ever since she had lain eyes on me as a shapeless pre-pubescent in my mother's hand-me-downs. My father laughed. Ha, the absurdity of it. He thought I was too good for Ah Bukien's son. 'That crazy antiquated relic thinks she's still living in Confucian times,' my father sneered. 'She doesn't realise that in this modern era parents don't arrange their children's hearts for them.'

*

Oh, I remembered the woman well. Once we went to her double-storey house in the centre of Footscray – the house she built from selling rice noodles. Every time my parents drove past that colossal mansion sitting smug between the dilapidated Victorian dwellings, they would point out the window and say, 'Look, there's Ah Bukien's rice-noodle house.' The day my parents decided to visit, I knew that it wasn't because they were particularly fond of seeing her. They only wanted to see her house. Ah Bukien had no problem with that arrangement – it was well established that Asian

236

acquaintances only ever visited each other to see their new homes anyway, just as it was an established rule that Asian youth never called their parents over the telephone just to chat. Any departure from these tacit protocols would arouse deep suspicions.

*

Ah Bukien was more than happy to give us her sedulously self-critical tour. 'See this,' she said, pointing a finger at a breathtakingly beautiful Chinese wooden table. 'My husband insisted that we buy it. I said to him, "Oh, you stupid man with your tragic countryside tastes, this looks like a godforsaken coffin I wouldn't even put our ancestral relics' toenail clippings in!" but the peasant insisted that we buy it, and do you know how much it cost? Do you? Have a guess. Guess.'

And so the rest of her house tour went on this way, with Ah Bukien lamenting the cost of every item her husband had insisted they purchase but first making us guess the price. My parents made sure their 'guesses' were sufficiently low enough but not *too* low. After Ah Bukien hurled out the real price, we all feigned courteous cardiac arrest and my mother would exclaim, 'Wah!' 'Wah indeed!' cried Ah Bukien. Later, in the car driving home, my mother chattered endlessly about Ah Bukien's abysmal taste and how shamelessly she showed everything off. 'And what about that carved coffin-table?' my father would exclaim. 'Her husband really is such a peasant.'

'I thought it was quite beautiful,' I said all of a sudden.

'You just watch it,' my mother warned me, 'you're beginning to acquire peasant tastes too.' My parents abhorred anything 'Oriental', anything that reminded them that we would grow up yellow and there was nothing they could do to save us.

*

I had never met Ah Bukien's boy. The day we visited her house, he was away being tutored. He had tutors for every subject. Ah Bukien showed off her son in the same way she showed off her assets. 'Woe, the school system here is not that good,' she told my mother one day.

'But sister,' my mother said (it was obligatory for my mother to call the older woman 'sister'), 'I thought you sent your son to a private school.'

'I did.' But the boy didn't make it into medicine. She was incensed that she couldn't even pay his way into the course. 'The boy is a retard!' *Indeed,* I wanted to add, *and this is the autistic boy you expect me to marry?* I didn't even know his name. I only knew him as 'Ah Bukien's son'. Her rice-noodle boy – quivery, white and malleable, made exactly like her pasta. I was resolute in hating him. Even if he were Adonis incarnate I would feel the same contempt towards him.

His sporting trophies were all lined up behind glass, in that heavy house of his. And his report card was mediocre in everything except physical education. That too was displayed behind the cabinet. I hated him even more – this was the type of boy who never gave me a second glance in high school, with my braces and ankle-length kilt. Except when they needed work from me. I suspected that he probably hated me too. That is, if he knew of his mother's intention. With all the pressure he was under, I wouldn't be surprised if her precious son was one of those boys who smoked pot behind the gymnasium in his blue blazer, going through life tormented by Oriental oedipal agonies.

When we were about to leave her house, Ah Bukien said to my parents, 'It is a pity you couldn't meet my son today.' Then she squeezed my cheeks until I could feel blood vessels erupting. The Cambodian Chinese liked their young girls to have cheeks as red as monkeys' bottoms. Already, she was endeavouring to mould me. Soon she even progressed to pinching me while I was at work.

*

At Footscray Retravision, there was a propensity for the mainland Chinese to refuse to buy items made in China. Whenever they said haughtily, '*O, zhongguo zuo de wo bu yao*' – I don't want anything made in China – I couldn't help myself. I would ask with salesgirl innocence, 'But sir, aren't *you* made in China?' Of course, I always had to feign that little giggle that sounded like two brightly coloured balloons rubbing rapidly up against each other. Unlike my younger sisters, who grew up with tastefully bland, tailor-made white and navy dresses, I spent my childhood with a grandmother who packaged me into padded Mao suits and made me sufficiently aware that I had to defend myself against all the other blandly dressed banana-children – children who were yellow on the outside but believed they could be completely white inside. My grandmother warned me that those children grew up to become sour, crumple-faced lemons. I believed her. That type manifested itself where I worked.

One day, I was explaining the functions of a Walkman to a customer when I felt someone twist the bare flesh of my upper arm. It hurt like hell. I turned around and there was that face – fierce eyes tattooed with permanent black liner, lashes sharpened with mascara. Every time she blinked, her eyes looked like two stygian insects in their death throes. 'Aghere!' she said in a too-loud voice. 'Are you working here for the holidays?'

No, I'm just loitering about trying to pinch something for my dope addiction. I'm intending to sell some to your tormented boy too. My pimp will be here any moment now.

'Yes, auntie,' I replied. 'Can I help you with anything?' I looked at her and knew she was one of those crude Asian mothers who tenaciously picked their noses in public – her nostrils were cavernous. I wondered what product she was enquiring about. Whatever question she was going to ask, I would direct her to another sales assistant. My Walkman customer was getting impatient. I looked at Ah Bukien expectantly.

'What was your Year 12 result?' she asked me.

I then realised that the product she was after was *me*. She was assessing my desirability for her son – it was a sick kind of transferred lasciviousness. Returning to my customer, I feigned indifference to her scrutiny, but secretly I relished the thought that if she was searching for my child-bearing hips she wouldn't find any.

Back at home, I told my parents with indignation about the pinch. 'She's just fond of you!' they laughed. Hell, if that was her way of showing affection, I wondered what she would do on my wedding night if she had her way. Probably hand her son a whip. She would make sure *everyone* attended her son's lavish banquet. I would be dressed in the same style as the Footscray wedding cake, crammed into a dress with too many frills, too much embroidery. No tasteful marzipan icing for Ah Bukien. No, I would be artificial cream fashioned into inedible roses. I would at least match their house.

And of course, true to established custom, I would have to move into Ah Bukien's household. Ideal daughters-in-law were meant to suffer stoically, but I refused to be the moribund butterfly, fluttering about helplessly, smashing Ming vases to sever some veins. I would not kowtow. My mother suffered for a decade under the rule of my grandmother, and she would not let me forget it. 'I hope that when you get married, you get a mother-in-law like the one I had!' she would yell whenever she wanted to throw the killer-curse on me.

I suspected that my mother was colluding with Ah Bukien. Both of them were plotting my descent into docility. There were generations of stupid women conspiring against my liberty, and there was no escape. When I was only a few months old, my mother cut off my eyelashes, believing they would grow back thicker and longer. She must have done it while I was asleep with a pair of nail scissors. As a baby, there was already a fault with me.

My mother was forever telling me to be careful. 'Careful' translated literally in Chinese means to have a 'small heart'. I refused to have a small heart. 'Why do so many boys call you?' my mother would ask after some boy had telephoned me. 'You're growing to be like Melanie.' My cousin Melanie was the family slut. There had to be one, and she was the first to develop large breasts, so she got stuck with the role.

By comparison I was still hermaphrodite-shaped. Nonetheless, Ah Bukien wanted me to go on a holiday with her son. 'Absolutely not!' retorted my father when my mother told him with relish. 'You know what she's after.' My father understood what it was like to have parents arrange things for their children. In Cambodia, my grandparents arranged a marriage for him with a girl who had a 'good' family background. He didn't love her and had no intention of marrying her. Unfortunately, that wasn't the case for her. I felt sorry for the poor girl. Her entire family had died under the Khmer Rouge. After the Pol Pot years, she followed my father all the way to Vietnam. 'Trailed behind him' was the way my mother put it, with a complacent scowl. 'What a disgraceful thing to do, following a young man around like a dog, when you were unwanted. Did she have no shame?'

*

Shame could be worse than death in my family, as I discovered. 'In Vietnam, when I was courting your mother,' my father told me one night in the car, 'I met your mother's eldest sister. And there was something very wrong with her. She could not talk to anybody. And everybody ignored her – none of her sisters would even acknowledge her. She didn't smile at all. She looked blank. I visited your mother often – and your auntie, once attractive and bright, was always that way afterwards. Blank. She was only young.'

I knew this was going to be a didactic story. 'What was wrong with her?'

'She fell in love with a man your grandmother didn't approve of. His family had a bad reputation.'

'So what happened?' I was intrigued. I didn't know much about my eldest auntie before, the only sister whose number my mother didn't keep in her phone book.

'Your grandmother beat her one night. And that's what made her go crazy.'

I wondered what my grandfather did while this was happening to his eldest daughter. I couldn't understand how any mother could beat her own child into lifelong depression just for falling in love with the wrong boy.

'She slept with him,' my father told me.

I didn't see my eldest auntie much, but ever since I could remember, the family had always referred to her as the 'crazy sister'. In all the years I had known her, I didn't think she was mad – but she was the most dejected person I had ever met. That beating three decades before had drained her of life. In photographs, she never smiled. Her face looked as if it were made of limp rubber. At family get-togethers, she was ignored. I remember reading the phrase 'life unworthy of life' somewhere. That was how my auntie was treated. There was no compassion for her – not even from her own family. I imagined that my grandmother would have told my auntie so many times in her youth to be careful. Not in the concerned 'don't get hurt' sense, but in the 'don't you *dare* bring shame on the family' sense.

*

'Be careful?' I wanted to retort. 'Mother, you risked gouging out my eyeballs when I was a baby just so I could blink at boys! And now you're telling me that if I don't be careful I am going to turn out a slut?' The Cambodians have a saying: 'A girl is like white cotton wool – once dirtied, it can never be clean again. A boy is like a gem – the more you polish it, the brighter it shines.'

Their plan was already working. Whenever I was alone with a boy I could not stop the guilty look over the shoulder. It became a reflex. I was already turning into the timid ingenue devoid of all personality that Asian women considered the consummate ideal. My head-swivelling compulsion unsettled most boys. 'What's the matter, Alice?' What could I tell them? 'Nothing, Benjamin, just checking to see if my parents are charging up from behind to attack you with a cleaver' or 'Don't worry, Andrew, I usually convulse from the neck up when I am in love.'

My family expected me to keep my eyes tightly shut until I was filed down to fine femininity. Anything I did of my own volition would shake up seven generations of dead ancestors and irrevocably damage the souls of the following seven. I couldn't care less about these stupid ancestors who were so resolute in crushing me. I dreamt of doing something that would make them turn in their graves and squish a decomposing eyeball.

*

This miscegenating rebel was doomed anyway. I was besotted with Edmund Johnson in my literature class. Tall and gangly Edmund: a Daniel Day-Lewis in paler hues. He had a liking for pure Chinese girls, not ones with origins from disease-ridden Third-World countries who couldn't even speak Mandarin. Yet he must have seen something 'exotic' in me. He probably 'liked' me in the way tourists were fascinated by the idiosyncratic charm of impoverished Asian villages. They were only there on holiday. He was a stupid tourist of the heart, I thought, he could be duped into liking anything 'foreign'.

I didn't realise until it was too late that he really *did* like me. By then I was crushed. Feeling too ugly, ungainly and undesirable for any boy, and devoid of all personality, I was just about ready to give up. Ah Bukien persisted with her insidious bartering. My parents ignored her entirely.

*

Every time we drove past that big white house in Footscray, I looked the other way and thought about Edmund. He had won a scholarship overseas for a year. He would literally be getting on a plane above me and going far, far away to a place where he could date purebred Mandarin girls with flaccid names like Peach Blossom and Lily Bloom to his heart's content.

I spent my summer holidays working at Retravision. One day there came a second pinch.

'Oh, auntie,' I said dully, still deep in my depressive torpor, 'what would you like?' Suddenly, my mother, who had also come to visit me at work, spotted Ah Bukien. They went to greet each other. I waited, pretending to dust electrical appliances so I could edge nearer to listen in on their conversation.

What does she have to say? I wondered. That her husband

bought her son and me a king-sized coffin of a bed? That she's paid for her son to study law or business?

'Oh, how are you, sister,' my mother asked. 'How is your husband? How is your house? How are your children? How are their studies going?'

Ah Bukien seemed to have lost her verbal virility for once. She didn't want to answer. Finally she sighed, 'My son doesn't go to school anymore.' I was stunned. In the ensuing silence, I pretended I was dusting a toaster.

'So what is he doing now?' my mother asked.

'Working at the factory.'

'What! You mean your rice noodle factory?'

'Yes.'

There was another silence. Then my mother responded quickly, 'Oh, it's good that he is already able to help you earn money! My daughter is a great woe to us, she has five years of law to go!'

'Well,' Ah Bukien finally said, 'she may not be earning you money now, but wait until she graduates!'

*

'Ah Bukien and I were just talking,' I heard my mother say to my father a little later. 'Her boy is already helping her earn money at the factory.'

'Oh, what a useful young man he is turning out to be!' smiled my father. I was incredulous at how skilled my parents were at this pretence. I knew they saw that there was no redemption for the boy. Suddenly, I felt very sorry for him. His mother had truly moulded him into the consummate rice-noodle boy. Yet she had firmly built him up to believe that the quiet, dark-eyed salesgirl at Retravision was his birthright, while my mother was bent on convincing me that, by disposition, girls were quivering martyrs.

The deep sad irony of this finally sunk in. If I believed that I was so ungainly and undesirable, there would be no need for me to be forever careful. I could go out at three o'clock in the morning and loiter around that suburb with the name that sounded like a coarse podiatric disease and nothing would happen to me. Ever. No news headline would read 'Young seventeen-year-old rebel violated and killed in Footscray'. I would be free.

LITTLE DUMPLINGS

On the island of Sitka, Alaska, the ships came into the port only once a week to replenish the food supply. With its white mist and black mountains, this land looked like the surface of a planet on a far-flung galaxy – Dante's Inferno frozen over, or Vesuvius after the rain of ash. I was here to conduct some writing workshops one winter, living in a house kindly loaned by some professors who were away. My front yard was a forest and my backyard was the edge of the bay that seeped into the Pacific Ocean. At night if I stood outside with my eyes wide open, the world looked exactly as if I had them closed. I wondered how I would get to food without a car. Above all, I began to worry about being too much alone.

One day Joan appeared at my front doorstep with a jar of home-made apple sauce. Her eyes, magnified behind concave glasses, were the colour of the Florida seascape. Joan was in her early sixties and my neighbour. She offered to drop me off every week at the local supermarket while she went to church. I had been living in the States for a few months now, and what I could not find in supermarkets in Iowa City or Florida or Poughkeepsie, I found in the mini-supermarket of Sitka: imported rice paper, fish sauce, sesame oil. I later discovered that people in this town cooked almost everything from scratch. Their kitchens were fully stocked with every herb and spice imaginable.

That afternoon, I made dumplings for Joan. Dumplings were my consummate comfort food. A few years back when I was living in China and feeling like a foreigner, I would go to the Peking University dumpling canteen and present my meal card for a plate of boiled dumplings. Eating them reminded me of sitting at the kitchen table at home with Mum, wrapping meat in pre-made skins from the Tatsing grocery store. At this time, the northern mainland Chinese and Uighurs had started to open dumpling houses across the road from the Footscray Market. Their fare was nothing as fancy as Hong Kong dim sum, and nowhere as complicated as Shanghai *xiao long bao* – little buns filled with broth inside. But these northern Chinese dumplings were shaped like ancient gold ingots, which was perhaps why they were traditionally served at Chinese New Year. The Chinese are obsessed with wealth. But they are also obsessed with humility, and this is personified by the dumpling – a modest white dough covering the good stuff: prawns, ginger, pork and scallions. A food that is more meat than flour and water.

When I first arrived in the States, I lived in the university town of Iowa City. After a couple of months of buffalo wings and fried mozzarella sticks, I craved dumplings so much that I began making them for my international friends. Vafo from Uzbekistan told me that they had a very similar food, and Millicent showed us how to make Jamaican *bwoil dumplin*. In Poughkeepsie Professor Ronald Sharp and his wife, Inese, also made dumplings with me. Professor Sharp folded his so that each dough ball seemed to have an enchanting edge of pleats like Victorian chair-leg skirts; while Inese made Latvian *piragi* that developed perfect tans in the oven. In Providence I made dumplings for Professor Smulyan because she had a cold and it seemed the equivalent of Jewish *matzo* soup.

Even in Sitka, there were no supermarket dumpling skins available, so I had to roll them from flour and water. I remembered a line from a Maxine Hong Kingston story, where the father would not eat dumplings because he claimed it was like eating the dirt from beneath women's fingernails. I chopped up spring onions and ginger, and used turkey meat because there seemed to be no such thing as minced pork in American supermarkets, it was all pre-seasoned sausage meat. Dumping them in a pot of boiling water, I watched the ingots float to the top like lifebuoys.

Standing on Joan's front doorstep with my plate, I was unsure whether a lady who made canned preserves would like this sort of stuff. I also worried whether she would trust a stranger's sense of personal hygiene. 'Come in! Come in!' she ushered. Joan was delighted. 'How wonderful! I will fry these up in butter.' She made a salad of beans and almonds. We served the dumplings with her home-made apple sauce. That strange and lovely fusion meal marked the beginning of our friendship, which grew into a rare amity where we would spend almost every day cooking and quilting and visiting craft shows bundled up in puffy coats, looking very much like the food that brought us together.

THE SHAPE OF THINGS
TO COME

A duct-tape dummy sounds like a device for sadomasochistic adult babies, but is actually an ingenious DIY invention you find online for creating a replica of your own torso. All you need is a coathanger, an old small t-shirt, polyester padding and three rolls of duct tape. You put on the t-shirt, your sister Alina wraps the tape around you and Nick cuts an opening down the back. Your silver casing peels off like the skin of a mummified Venus de Milo. Hanging it on the coathanger, you stuff it with the guts of an old pillow and seal up the back, armholes and bottom with more duct tape. You know it doesn't look like a Lincraft haberdashery mannequin, but you are getting married in less than two months, and you're not going to sweat the small details.

'Writing is a profession for introverts who want to tell you a story but don't want to make eye contact while doing it,' says John Green. This story is not one of love at first sight, or second sight, foresight or even hindsight. You first meet the man who will become your husband at college. He is eighteen and comes from a valley six hours' drive away. He can't get used to how easily everyone can talk about ideas, and how fast they think. You want to tell him that some of these students don't even do their own laundry – they take it to their parents' home on weekends. One day Nick takes his blender into the city for repair. You thought that everyone knew small appliances had a built-in obsolescence; but back in his rural hometown, things were built to last, like the Snowy Mountains hydro scheme.

Nick is allocated the smallest room but doesn't mind because he'd always shared a room with his brothers. You'd also shared not only a room but also a big double bed, first with your grandma, then with your younger brother and finally with your sisters. So you become intoxicated by your newfound independence.

Life is too interesting to be interrupted by romance, too filled with things to do and a feral vitality to write, to be hindered and trapped and monopolised by the thoughts and feelings of another human being. That's how you saw marriage and children then, because this was how it was experienced in your family: your father was the pioneer but your mother was locked out of the world by her lack of language and four kids.

Nick is a quiet man. You have no idea what colour his eyes are because he always looks at his hands when he speaks to anyone. You don't find out until six years later, when you are giving a talk at Box Hill library. You see a familiar young face amid a sea of kindly geriatric faces. He'd recently returned from his travels around the world working on farms, and had come along with his grandparents. You arrange to meet up, which eventually leads to an evening dinner of roast and Yorkshire pudding at his grandparents' house, where they also show you the oyster mushrooms he is growing in their garage.

You had dated people who wanted to talk all the time, to the point where you found yourself quietly holding your breath, thinking about Gibran's lines:

You talk when you cease to be at peace with your thoughts;
And when you can no longer dwell in the solitude of your heart
you live in your lips,

and sound is a diversion and a pastime.

And in much of your talking, thinking is half murdered.

With Nick, you feel peace instead of excitement, calm instead of anxiety. A friend wrote to you saying that that kind of feeling was not falling in love, it was 'falling in relief'. But at thirty, you can hear your own thoughts again.

And that's when you know.

Here is a man who can mix concrete, pour foundations, cut logs, kill spiders and mice, drive tractors, grow things, keep bees and work cattle. He is a doer and not a talker, and he doesn't ridicule your duct-tape dummy. He also doesn't bat an eyelid when you lug home a Salvation Army bag and tell him, 'I've finally found it.'

The bag contains a $60 massive meringue 1980s frock covered in hand-beaded lace: the very same stuff you saw in a boutique fabric store for hundreds of dollars a metre.

It seemed too easy to go into a shop to buy a gown. Maybe that's why they made it so hard for you – an appointment weeks in advance, a container to stand on, two women pinning down folds of fabric behind you so you look like a battle-weary Barbie out of her box. You see a grown woman on another box cry. Who cries over a dress when all they've had to do was hand over the credit card? They didn't have to make a stitch of the damn thing, prick their fingers embroidering fake pearls, worry about their toddler inhaling glass beads or getting asthma from being in the garage for too long while they sewed.

You are out of there in twenty minutes.

Nick's mother tells you that her mother made her wedding gown. Your mother never had a 'big day', or a dress. You have a sneaking suspicion that the term 'classy' was invented by people with no sartorial imagination, and these same people invented 'tacky' to make fun of the loveliest things poor people could afford. Both mothers are not vain women. They wear flat shoes and barely any make-up. Nick's father fixes farming equipment, your father repaired watches. Nick's mother grows vegetables and knits blankets, your mother preserves pickles and hems her own sheets.

But a big difference between the two mums is that your mum is fanatically superstitious. If she finds out you'd bought a second-hand wedding gown and are intending to cut it up, she'd probably go off the rails. 'Sharp objects bring terrible luck! And how do you know this dress doesn't come with a terrible history?' But that's exactly how your talented beautician aunty lost her livelihood – no Asian bride wanted to get their face made up by her after her divorce. You also know that your family comes with its own terrible history, as all refugees do; yet that doesn't stop Nick from wanting to be part of your life.

Also, your family don't own anything old. The killing fields made sure of that. There are no family heirlooms, only family stories. You don't want to tell your kids that their dad handed over a little square of plastic for a coveted material thing. You want them to understand how to work with, and transform, real material. You want to tell them that for four weeks, you and their dad sat together every evening while he read and you stitched, and you both talked. You want to tell your children that their father is still full of surprise and mystery. But for now, you drape the oversized, second-hand dress on the duct-tape dummy, and think with wonder and joy about the shape of things to come.

TWO CULTURES
AND A BABY

'What are you doing?' my hospital roommate asks. I'm standing by the door of our shared bathroom, towel in hand, waiting for the nurse to return with a shower cap. In antenatal classes I was told a warm shower is comforting when going into labour, but I don't want to give birth with wet hair dripping down my back.

'No, no, no,' my roommate insists, 'you must wash your hair now!' I'd only met the woman a few moments ago, through the curtained partition separating our beds, when I walked over to the bathroom as my contractions began. 'Didn't your mum teach you? You can't wash your hair for thirty days after you have a baby, so you must do it now. This is your last time!' I smile and thank her for her advice, then slink back to my side of the room. She has a Thai accent, and I know exactly what she is talking about, but pretend not to. I also know that she will sequester herself in her heated house for at least thirty days after giving birth, refrain from washing her hair, maybe not even shower, and live on a diet of special soups and tonics.

Every pregnant woman, and new parent, receives their fair dose of unsolicited advice from well-intentioned family members and strangers. Most of it is mildly annoying, but some of it can be anxiety-inducing, particularly if you feel you have to pretend to follow that advice to alleviate the concerns of loved ones whose fears you don't share yourself. The Chinese and South-East Asian practice of *zuo yue zi*, which literally means 'sitting the month', goes back thousands of years and is even mentioned in the *I Ching*. Hospitals in Australia make allowance for this practice, which they refer to as 'cultural confinement', by sending nurses to visit the postpartum mother, who is not allowed outside the house. There are other things a new mother is not supposed to do: drink cold drinks, squat, eat certain vegetables and fruit, stand by an open window, turn on air-conditioning or cry.

Not every mother will follow all of these rules, and they vary in different regions of Asia. Other cultures also practise postpartum confinement – South Americans, Indians and traditional Greeks, for instance – but the distinct practices of my heritage spread from the north of China to the warmer climes of South-East Asia. My family are ethnic Chinese, born in Cambodia, and I think a lot of the theory behind the customs must have got lost in translation. Much of it seems like superstitious claptrap, especially when I remember my grandmother prohibiting my pregnant aunt from watching cartoons with us because she didn't want the unborn baby to come out 'deformed' like Alvin the Chipmunk. Whenever nurses ask whether I will practise cultural confinement, I tell them definitely not.

Nonetheless, during my pregnancy I developed a heightened awareness of the fragility of life. I was grateful when friends gave me bags of baby clothes from their own children, but I could not sort through them or look at them. *Just in case.* I couldn't digest the idea of a baby shower. *Just in case.* Because I was so nauseous for the first three months, I was filled with feelings of catastrophic expectancy. Conceived in a refugee camp and naturally under-weight all my life, I wasn't confident that I could grow a healthy and robust baby. I kept my fears to myself, yet with every doctor and midwife visit, I also realised how seriously the medical profession took the possibility of pre- and postnatal depression. My sister, who is a doctor, told me that some suffering mothers at the hospital wouldn't pick up their babies or feed them.

Ever since I was twenty, one motherhood image has inadvertently and continually flashed through my mind: a photograph of a mother holding her baby in a strange way. The photo was from the Tuol Sleng Genocide Museum in Phnom Penh, Cambodia. Meticulous in their documentation of death, the Khmer Rouge took photos of every prisoner before they executed them. The mother holds her prostrate newborn low, almost near her waist. She stares straight at the camera, the ultimate face of detachment.

At the hospital, I collected the beyondblue booklet *A Guide to Emotional Health and Wellbeing During Pregnancy and Early Parenthood*, but I also wondered whether there was one for new grandparents. All the terrible things that could happen, my parents expected to happen, with the only insurance being that I stay home all the time, only venturing to and from work. 'Don't go to Little Saigon Market in Footscray,' Mum warned me. 'You'll slip over fruit scraps on the ground, fall and miscarry.'

My parents cannot accept pain as part of my life. It seems to make them suffer more than it actually makes me suffer. They worry all the time, and in their old age it seems to have gotten worse. Their anxiety is physical and palpable: it scatters their thoughts and makes my mother break out with a nasty rash all over her limbs. From time to time, she also suffers from debilitating depression. My father still weighs around 45 kilograms. During the Khmer Rouge years, they lost everything – first their families, and then their possessions; understandably, their world has narrowed to a few concentric circles, the pivotal one in the centre being their children, the second their electrical appliance business. They have always been overprotective of us to a pathological degree. As author Helen Motro explains through her studies of Holocaust survivors:

> Not all of our fathers beat their sons … Not all of our mothers froze us out as teenagers because they themselves survived by abandoning their own mothers at 15 in the camps. No, most of us had parents who loved too much, who smothered us with their care, their solicitude, their ever-present, all-enveloping anxiety.

There's a specific brand of anxiety, called 'transgenerational trauma', that affects those with genocide-affected parents. Studies have even shown that children of Jewish Holocaust survivors have altered levels of circulating stress hormones compared to other adults of the same age. They simultaneously feel overprotected *by* their parents and overprotective *of* their parents. All grandchildren are joys to their grandparents, but this first grandchild means something more to my father, who has seen the death of so many children he knew and loved. Although he never directly mentions this feeling of loss, my father has always spoken with yearning of having 'four generations under one roof', the ultimate Chinese idea of a blessed family.

*

I am in a room in the physiotherapy department at the Royal Women's Hospital in Melbourne with ten other women. We've all been referred by our doctors, midwives and, in some cases, social workers. We range from our late teens to our early forties, first-time mothers, second-time mothers, Turkish, Scottish, Scandinavian, and even a mum who identifies as Gypsy. I only know this because during the introduction we were asked to say our names and explain how we got them. We are all strangers to one another but the anonymity is comforting. We don't share personal stories, because this is not therapy.

When I had mentioned to my hospital midwife some of my worries, she enrolled me in the hospital's antenatal mindfulness course. The five-week Mind Baby Body group-learning program is facilitated by a perinatal psychiatrist, Dr Kristine Mercuri, who explains that anxiety is the most common ailment of pregnancy. Six years ago, the hospital paid for mindfulness-trained practition-ers to run programs for oncology patients. Kristine then devised a similar program for pregnant women. She had studied under Professor Jon Kabat-Zinn, the creator of the Mindfulness-Based Stress Reduction program that is used in hospitals worldwide, who defines mindfulness as 'paying attention in a particular way: on purpose, in the present moment, and non-judgmentally'.

Kabat-Zinn's original mindfulness program is eight weeks long, requiring one to two hours' practice per day. This program is shorter, Kristine says, because 'I couldn't ask pregnant women who are already so busy to commit to this level of practice. Yet the great thing about pregnancy is that there's a deadline, and having this deadline focuses women's attention. And if they are paying atten-tion and focused, their practice will be concentrated.'

We're all sitting on the floor, a large plastic mat spread out in front of us, holding ice cubes in our hands, as many as we can fit into each fist. Kristine advises us when to let go of them, and when to pick them up again. First, we hold the ice for sixty seconds. It's a cold day and the ice stings my palms, but when we're allowed to let go, my fingers feel suddenly suffused with warmth, and I exhale with relief.

Kristine draws a diagram on the whiteboard of a series of peaked hills. She explains that these represent labour contractions, with crests being the height of pain and the dips the reprieves. 'Most people are scared of pain, so in between the pain they worry about the next wave and tense up,' she says, 'but if you learn how to be in the present moment, you will not fear the pain.' After a sixty-second reprieve, Kristine instructs us to pick up the ice again, but this time to breathe into the stinging sensations. We are encouraged to count our breath, make a low humming voice, even smile. The more aware I am of the pain – noticing that it comes in waves – the less energy I waste in fighting it.

'When you go into labour, cover the clock,' she suggests, 'because you have no control over how long your labour will take.' Kristine says that birth plans were originally intended to give women back control over the medicalisation of their delivery, but they can set up unrealistic expectations. 'Your bodies know what to do,' she reassures. 'It's growing a baby without your mind having to direct itself to it.'

The program was originally intended to help women deal with the pressures of impending parenthood and pregnancy, but Kristine discovered that a lot of expectant mothers also wanted coping techniques to deal with giving birth.

'The present moment is the only time you can make appropriate decisions,' Kristine explains. 'People who remain present under pressure will make better choices, instead of reacting automatically based on past experiences.'

In our final session, when Kristine takes the roll, one of the mothers in the group is already in the labour ward. We finish off with a 'loving-kindness' exercise before we go our separate ways.

After the first trimester, the rest of my pregnancy is a surprisingly happy time. There are moments of worry, of course, like getting food poisoning and an eight-day migraine. There are moments of annoyance, such as being told off by my mother for transgressions I don't understand, like walking faster than a geriatric shuffle or eating walnuts. But, on the whole, each day brings more and more energy and optimism. Sitting alone in my flat one afternoon, I have the unassailable feeling that things will work out, and, if not, then I am resilient enough to cope. I still feel a little like I have been carrying the 'replacement' for lost relatives, but rather than a burden, it now feels a comfort.

I'd begun the Mind Baby Body program as emotional insurance against postnatal depression. What I did not expect is how the mindfulness practice suddenly comes to fruition when I go into labour.

My waters break on a Saturday evening after dinner at my parents' house. Nick and I return home, I pack a bag and we walk to the Royal Women's Hospital, feeling excited anticipation. Something is happening, and when it does happen, it is not the worst pain I've ever had in my life. Who knew that forty-five minutes holding melting ice in my hands could prepare me so well for the next five hours? In labour, you realise how finite your energy is. I don't want to waste it by crying, so I start humming instead, louder with each increasing wave. I know I must sound ridiculous to the Thai woman in the next bed, the one who insisted that I wash my hair, but I no longer care. I now understand why monks chant and cows moo. Someone arrives – I wonder if it is the nurse with the shower cap. 'The nurse told me that I'd find a very happy singing patient in Bed 21,' the midwife says when she sees me, 'and she was right.'

Our baby is born at thirty-five weeks, but when he is put on my chest, I don't understand that he is premature and small. Because I am also small, he seems a perfect size for me. He's a strange creature, looking up at me with one grey eye and two yellow eyebrows, one curiously raised. The other eye is stuck shut.

Marvelling over his matted black hair and miniature nipples, I cannot believe that this little person folded inside me has come out in one piece. I am euphoric. I look at Nick, battle-weary, still holding my hand. Like an Olympic runner I've been fully concentrating on getting through the task, but patient Nick had to wait out the protracted minutes and hours as a spectator.

When the nurse takes our baby upstairs to the Newborn Intensive and Special Care (NISC) unit, my midwife, Ellen, gets me a sandwich and helps me into the shower afterwards. Just like my mum thirty-four years ago, when she gave birth to me, I cannot believe the kindness of the hospital staff. As a new mother, I am luckier, though – the nurses are looking after my baby in intensive care, I can eat the hospital food and keep it down (Mum couldn't stomach Western food at first) and, most importantly, I can speak English. My mother once told me that when I was born and she was left alone in the room with me, I wouldn't stop crying. Her milk hadn't come in yet and she had no idea what to do, so she fed me Nescafé with sweetened condensed milk from a plastic spoon.

In the Victorian public hospital system, if the mother is healthy and fit, she will go home after one night's stay. Ellen takes me to my room and tells me to rest, that a nurse will check on me soon. When the nurse comes, she hands me a card with our baby's bed number. She says that if I can't breastfeed him, I should still be waking up every two to three hours to hand-express milk for him. A physiotherapist comes with some handouts about pelvic floor and abdominal exercises, and advises me to begin them as soon as I can. Then a pharmacist comes with a sheet of medications and vitamins I should take. A final nurse comes and tells me about wound care, and about correct sleeping techniques for the baby to prevent cot death.

'What if you have a patient who can't read?' I ask her, taking the handouts she gives me.

'Well, then you'd have real difficulty,' she acknowledges, 'but we do have some translators.'

The staff at the hospital are kind, helpful and, as I can see, often stretched to their limit with the endless rotation of birthing patients. I am in very good shape, so am discharged from the hospital two days later. I walk home from the hospital with Nick, feeling a little sorry to leave, my bag heavy with printed instructions.

Our baby stays in the NISC for another week. He is in a humidicrib, and two days after his birth he has a feeding tube put in his nose because his blood glucose level is low. I wake up at six in the morning and visit him until 11 at night. I am there so he can have a feed every three hours, and I also hold him against my chest so we can bond. It feels a lot like falling in love, but without the agitation or self-doubt. For that one week I am lucky enough to do nothing but *be* with my baby. I'm also lucky enough to be able to return home and sleep through the night, while he is in the expert hands of the nurses. I walk home, grateful for our public health system and happy to be a taxpayer. *Tax away*, I think, *if this is the kind of treatment every mother and child gets.*

After the birth of a baby, a mother home from hospital usually has to entertain visitors, disrupting both her own and the baby's sleep, and his feeds. But only two people at a time are allowed in the NISC unit. My parents are regular visitors. My mother brings me food at the hospital every morning before she catches a train to work. She is comforted by the sterile ward, the room with six baby beds and the rotating nurses, the humidicrib. Nothing like this existed in the Cambodia she grew up in.

As I have to walk to and from the hospital early in the morning and late at night, my parents must resign themselves to accept it.

I realise that they are likely getting some degree of tacit opprobrium from our small community and relatives. *How could they let a daughter out of the house in the cold? How could they let her walk home from the hospital after giving birth?*

When Kate Middleton brought baby George out to the front steps of the hospital to show the world, the tone of Chinese and Taiwanese media coverage of the event was not of excitement, but grave alarm. Chinese medical 'experts' on the news weighed in on what possible harm she could cause herself and her child, being outdoors so soon.

My mother does not mention a word about me 'sitting the month'. Instead, she keeps bringing me food: pig's trotter soup with ginger, chicken soup with goji berries and ginseng, braised eggs, salmon, and litres and litres of PhysiCAL milk. All these things, she says, are to help me recover and produce more breast-milk, but when I ask how they work, she just mutters something about warming the blood.

'Remember not to read anything during this time,' she repeatedly warns. 'You could damage your eyes.' I don't tell her about all the instructional booklets and brochures the hospital has given me. 'Don't move too much or squat,' she instructs, 'because you'll become incontinent later in life.' I don't tell her about the physiotherapist who encouraged pelvic floor exercises immediately. Whenever my mother sees me at the hospital, I am in a big red chair with my baby on my chest, either feeding him or warming him like a human heat pod. This sedentary existence pleases her immensely.

In hospital our baby was buffered by nurses, doctors, midwives and a sanitised environment; when he comes home a week later both Nick and I fall ill with colds, which we cannot help but pass on to him. Fortunately, it does not weaken his sucking reflex. I am in our bedroom nursing our baby when my mother suddenly barges in. 'You can't just lie there all day feeding him. Your face is all shrunken and drained!' She demands that I pull the baby off the breast, get out of bed and immediately eat the soup she has brought. I tell her I've already had Weet-Bix for breakfast, and she yells at me for that, loud enough to startle the baby so that he unlatches from me. 'You never listen to me,' she scolds. 'You'll make your baby sick and then you'll be sorry! And why is the heater turned up so high? You'll suffocate him!' Her tirade goes on and on. Annoyed, I growl at her to stop hassling me. My mother is a series of contradictions: she wants me to stay warm but now we're *too life-threateningly* warm; she was happy to see me feed the baby in the hospital but now she wants him exclusively weaned on the bottle; and she wants me to eat grains but not breakfast cereal!

'It's just a cold,' I tell her. 'We'll get over it.'

When my mother leaves I keep feeding the baby in our heated room, but after I finish I eat her soup.

A week later, the rest of our relatives come to visit. Nick's family make the five and a half hour drive from Corryong to marvel over the little miracle and are content holding him, but my family dispense endless advice. I shouldn't go out, now that I'm safely ensconced in our flat. My father instructs Nick to make sure I eat enough, because he says Asian women are weaker (which chagrins me, but amuses my husband). My eldest aunty makes me a fig, goji berry and white fungi soup. Aunty Kieu brings us pork dumplings, and Aunty Ly makes me a sweet potato pudding. Aunty Sim tells me to eat peanuts to increase milk production. I am barely alone, but never have to 'entertain' family; instead, they hold the baby so I can eat all the food they have brought. They bottle-feed the baby so I can rest. My mother comes over every day bearing soups infused with Chinese medical herbs.

Although postnatal depression is a debilitating and real condition, I wonder how much of the baby blues can be attributed to an unexpected detrimental change in circumstances. Reading Naomi Wolf's *Misconceptions*, I imagine a poor young Anglo-Australian mum at home looking at Miranda Kerr's postnatal abdominals in *Woman's Day*, in between having to breastfeed her baby (sometimes above a new C-section wound), cook, clean and deal with visitors who want to wake the baby up to look at the colour of his eyes. When everyone leaves, she feels neglected and isolated in her house, with only a bag of hospital booklets to guide her until the next visit from the maternal and child health nurse, booklets advising her to breastfeed and exercise immediately.

In contrast, through their visits, food and endless advice, my family make sure I understand that I am equally important as the baby, if not more so: to be his primary caregiver I have to be in optimal health. I realise that my family have inherited a great lore of nutritional wisdom that they often can't explain, knowledge I once dismissed as quackery. When I have a cold or sore throat, I know to boil Lo Han Guo (*siraitia grosvenorii*) in water to make a tea. I know about the inherent 'heating' and 'cooling' properties of some foods. And we were putting goji berries and red dates in our soups before they became 'superfoods'. When I had a severe asthma attack at my uncle's house and had left my Ventolin at home, he gave me a bag of herbs to inhale, which miraculously cleared my lungs. During the Pol Pot years, when my father was surviving the killing fields, his acupuncture skills – the practice performed with thick copper electrical wires he found on the side of the road – cured village chiefs with stomach aches, and children whose limbs flopped listlessly to their sides after being tied for too long in punishment. I can't believe that I was once afraid that they'd *impose* their ways onto *my modern* motherhood and *my modern* baby.

Yet what happens to all the new Asian mothers who do not have their parents around, or whose parents are still overseas? Getting statistics on the number of women practising confinement in Australia is similar to trying to work out how many people celebrate Greek Orthodox Easter or practise Bikram yoga. For Chinese in mainland China, Taiwan and South-East Asia, however, it's a cultural norm, and confinement nannies can be hired to cook special meals for the new mum, take care of the newborn, even do the housework and laundry. Mothers can even check into confinement clinics, where they spend the month recuperating. Top clinics can charge up to $US500 per day. In Australia, such services are harder to come by, although individual older women might advertise their services as confinement nannies in the local ethnic newspapers, and Chinese medical practitioners can prepare special herbs for postpartum mothers.

The only Australian company I can find that offers a more holistic care model is Confinement Care in Sydney, run by the husband-and-wife team of Eric Cheng and Anni Chien. Anni is a qualified and registered Chinese-medicine practitioner specialising in pregnancy care, while Eric is an educator.

They set up Confinement Care after witnessing the pregnancies of their friends who were receiving good support through the conventional public and private healthcare system. 'But when these couples started thinking about their postnatal plans, those who grew up in families with strong Chinese heritage suddenly realised that information was not so clear-cut, and often confusing,' Eric explains. After growing increasingly frustrated over some of the 'poorly informed postnatal practices that mothers were putting themselves in', Eric and Anni developed a service that provides new mothers with acupuncture, meal plans, advice and even herbal sachets for soups and baths. Yes, baths.

Eric explains that the practice of not washing for thirty days after giving birth originated in northern China, where winters were harsh and washing was conducted in riversides and near communal wells, in an era plagued with water-borne diseases such as cholera. 'Washing in these environments contradicts Chinese medical advice, as it creates moments of vulnerability for pathogens to attack the body,' Eric explains. 'At some point in time, this guidance was removed from its context and adapted as a blanket rule. But obviously we are not exposed to waterborne viruses in our tap water, and we do not experience sudden fluctuations in temperature as we bath and shower in enclosed and heated bathrooms. Given these reasons, this "rule" should not apply to mothers in Australia.' Eric mentions that there are other superstitious practices that draw on people's fear of non-compliance, some purely based on the way similar words sound in certain dialects.

But these rituals distract from the real rationale for confinement. 'When we talk about postnatal "confinement",' Eric explains, 'we are referring to a time that is intentionally set aside for three purposes: to rest and recover from pregnancy and the birthing process, to build a healthy body to begin the motherhood journey, and to create ample opportunities for mother and baby to bond. It is somewhat unfortunate that translators have appointed unglorifying terms like 'confinement', 'sitting month', or even 'doing the month', leading people to think the focus is on restriction and non-movement, and that it is to be endured.

'Clinically, women who do not have a good recovery often suffer postnatal issues like severe fatigue, lower back pain, insomnia and hair loss. These can often last for months or even years after the pregnancy.'

Indeed, this diagnosis accords with the World Health Organization's observations that the puerperium – the six weeks following birth – is a critical period, as most maternal and infant deaths occur during this time.

Eric also mentions the importance of 'reassuring anxious new grandparents', something Western healthcare fails to address because of different familial structures. 'If intergenerational conflict does arise over confinement approaches, the new father should step in to protect the mother's wellbeing, and help remove the unsaid expectation that the daughter or daughter-in-law has to sacrifice her personal needs for the sake of harmony with the older generation.'

In becoming a mother, I've found I've also become a different daughter. My parents' overwhelming anxious love was once a burden, and as a young adult I was either fighting or fleeing it. As a young mother, I have been unexpectedly freed from worry: the more my parents fret over our baby, the more I am able to choose to be a calm parent, to understand that this is not an innate temperament, but a feeling of safety derived from secure and comfortable circumstances. It is a gift.

When we take our baby to visit his great-grandparents, my 83-year-old grandmother tells me to drink wine with every meal. 'It warms the *qi*,' she says. 'If you can afford it, buy the wine with the most alcohol content.' When she gave birth to her eight children, she had to make do with homemade rice wine. 'It was cheaper.' She also notices our baby has a milky-white tongue, and suggests that I give him a cloth to bite on as a remedy. 'Ma, they don't do peasanty things like that anymore!' scoffs my mum to her own mother.

My grandma tells me that when she had her children, a tin of formula was $9. My grandfather made $10 a day as a cook. He gave a dollar to each kid at the end of the day, and the parents each kept one for themselves. So of course they could not afford formula milk. Instead, my grandmother bought Nestlé sweetened condensed milk and diluted it with water. 'A milk bottle with a teat was $20,' she tells me, 'so I got a Coke bottle and poked a hole through the lid!' She is delighted by her own ingenuity. I come to understand that my forebears were not silly and superstitious: illiteracy and poverty robbed them of proper nutrition, and they were all just doing their best to make the next generation better and stronger. Having two cultures with very different approaches to childbirth and motherhood has made me more relaxed, knowing that there is no right way to do things.

In my grandparents' house, I look at my baby's father, who is kind, calm and fearless, and hope that our child will have enough of his genes to cancel out my history of fear. I look at my grandma and 95-year-old grandpa, who came to Cambodia as starving peasants from China and ended up in Australia in their twilight years, surviving together through sixty years of marriage, delighting over our son. And I look at my own mother, proudly bottle-feeding the baby with formula milk that she never would have been able to have as a baby herself. We are four generations under one roof again.

AFTERWORD & ACKNOWLEDGEMENTS

When I was about nineteen, I began writing short stories and submitting them to publications. Eventually I had one published in *Meanjin*. An editor at Black Inc., Chris Feik, read the story and gave me a call out of the blue. 'You've got an interesting and unique voice. Your story sounds like it's a part of a novel. Is it?'

At the age of nineteen I wasn't very good at short stories, so my story probably sounded unfinished.

And I said, 'Yes. Yes, it is.'

He responded, 'Great, I'd love to see some chapters.'

I replied, 'Sure. They're a bit rough, so I'll just edit them and bring them over.'

I didn't have any chapters, so I sat down and wrote 30,000 words. At first I wasn't even going to visit Chris, but one evening I saw the movie *Frieda* with two friends. I realised how brave Frieda was. She brought her paintings to Diego Rivera and said, 'Hey, Diego, you want to look at my paintings?' I thought, *Maybe I'll show Chris my stories.* I didn't even call him for an appointment – I didn't know how these things worked at that age. I just walked into his office. Chris left a meeting to accept my stories, which were presented in a font that I thought was classy but was perhaps ridiculous.

I knew I didn't have enough words for a novel yet, so I asked, 'Can I send you a story every month, to get me writing? You don't have to read it. You just keep it in your inbox.'

So I sent him stories until he said, 'Stop. Let's put them together in a book.'

That book became *Unpolished Gem.*

A great editor is like a great chef – they often work with raw ingredients, and it is almost by alchemy that work is transformed, essential truths are discovered and themes realised. A great editor will often know your work better than you do. They notice your recurring obsessions with a clarity that you, through your subjectivity, lack. When Chris wrote to me last year suggesting this collection, I wasn't sure I had written enough over the years to justify a book. But I trust Chris's judgement. It was he who took a risk on this unknown writer who'd barely ventured beyond Melbourne's western suburbs, let alone into the world.

Chris Feik and Julia Carlomagno have curated these stories and essays, spanning one and a half decades of my writing life, from my first published piece, 'Unpolished Gem' (2001), to my most recent, 'Home Truths' (2017). They have arranged them in a way that tells not only the story of my development as a writer, but also the story of a family, a suburb, a country and a world over a particular time.

My focus has always been on character and on narrative voice. I've never been interested in interviewing 'powerful' people who presume (or pretend) to know the answers. Perhaps the opposite of faith is not doubt but certainty, and I don't believe in fixed positions and the irrevocable power of words. After all, my own mother has never read anything I have written. She can't read, and her life is no less rich or devoid of meaning. So these pages mostly contain stories of ordinary people, who offer – sometimes inadvertently – unusual insights.

I've always had faith in the power of a good story, not a didactic story, to shift one's view about people and places that are often misunderstood or maligned, and I am thankful to all the people in this anthology who've generously shared their time and trust with this writer.

Alice Pung, 2018

PUBLICATION DETAILS

'24/7' first appeared in *The Monthly*, October 2008.

'Against Calamitous Odds' first appeared as the introduction to Ruth Park's *Swords and Crowns and Rings*, Text Publishing, Melbourne 2012.

'Ally of the Dolls' first appeared in *The Monthly*, December 2008 – January 2009.

'Caveat Emptor' first appeared in *The Monthly*, October 2013.

'Chinese New Year Dragon' first appeared in *Good Weekend*, 2006.

'Dark Fiction' first appeared in *The Guardian*, 2 October 2017.

'Executing History' first appeared in Nataša Ďurovičová with Hugh Ferrer (eds), *Fall and Rise, American Style*, 91st Meridan Books, Iowa, 2015.

'Hair Apparent' first appeared in *The Monthly*, July 2010.

'Holiday at Slacks Creek' first appeared in *The Australian*, 1 March 2008.

'Home Truths' first appeared in *The Monthly*, December 2017 – January 2018.

'It's Time to Embrace the "F" Word' first appeared in *The Age*, October 2007.

'Katharine's Place' first appeared in *The Monthly*, July 2008.

'Letter to A' first appeared in *Best Australian Stories 2007*, Black Inc., Melbourne, 2007.

'Little Dumplings' first appeared in *The Age*, 13 March 2010.

'Living with Racism' first appeared in *The New York Times*, 7 December 2016.

'Looking Sheepish' first appeared in *The Monthly*, February 2009.

'Mum in the Forbidden City' first appeared in *The Lifted Brow*, August 2011.

'Opportunity' first appeared in *The Monthly*, March 2008.

'Returning' first appeared in *The Lifted Brow*, October 2013.

'School Days' first appeared in *The Monthly*, May 2009.

'Screen Dumps' first appeared in *The Lifted Brow*, April 2011.

'Searching for Ai Hua in America' first appeared in *The Lifted Brow*, February 2011.

'Shunned in a Strange Land' first appeared in *The Sydney Morning Herald*, 17 August 2008.

'Silence of the Phones' first appeared in *The Monthly*, April 2008.

'Spirit Chimes' first appeared in *The Age*, 3 October 2009.

'Stealing from Little Saigon' first appeared in *Joyful Strains: Making Australia Home*, Affirm Press, Melbourne 2013.

'STOP RACE MIXING!' first appeared in the Australia-Indonesia Centre essay series, October 2016.

'Strawberry Fields Forever' first appeared in *Good Weekend*, 11 November 2006.

'The Bus' first appeared in Susan La Marca and Pam MacIntyre (eds), *Where the Shoreline Used to Be*, Penguin Books, Melbourne, 2007.

'The Field Marker' first appeared in *Griffith Review*, October 2010.

'The Flashing Green Man' first appeared in *The Age*, 12 January 2012.

'The Secret Life of Them' first appeared in *The Monthly*, February 2013.

'The Shed' first appeared in *A Journal of Learning*, 22 July 2012.

'The Winter After the Olympics' first appeared in *Strange Flowers: Australia-China Encounters in Writing and Art*, Wakefield Press, 2011.

'Throwing the Book' first appeared in *The Monthly*, August 2007.

'Two Cultures and a Baby' first appeared in *The Monthly*, June 2015.

'Unpolished Gem' first appeared in *Meanjin*, vol. 61, no. 1, 2002.

'Who is the Ordinary Reasonable Person?' first appeared in *The Monthly*, May 2014.

'Writing about My Father' first appeared in *Westerly*, vol. 72, no. 2, 2012.